OPPOSING
VIEWPOINTS®
SERIES

Religion in
Contemporary Society

Other Books of Related Interest

Opposing Viewpoints Series

America's Changing Demographics
Identity Politics
Race in America
Sanctuary Cities
Western Democracy at Risk

At Issue Series

The Death Penalty
Domestic Terrorism
The Role of Religion in Public Policy
The Role of Science in Public Policy
Vaccination

Current Controversies Series

Are There Two Americas?
Freedom of Speech on Campus
Political Correctness
The Political Elite and Special Interests
Political Extremism in the United States

"Congress shall make no law … abridging the freedom of speech, or of the press."

First Amendment to the US Constitution

The basic foundation of our democracy is the First Amendment guarantee of freedom of expression. The Opposing Viewpoints series is dedicated to the concept of this basic freedom and the idea that it is more important to practice it than to enshrine it.

OPPOSING
VIEWPOINTS®
SERIES

Religion in
Contemporary Society

Avery Elizabeth Hurt, Book Editor

GREENHAVEN
PUBLISHING

Published in 2022 by Greenhaven Publishing, LLC
353 3rd Avenue, Suite 255, New York, NY 10010

Cover image: Rawpixel.com/Shutterstock.com

Library of Congress Cataloging-in-Publication Data
Names: Hurt, Avery Elizabeth, editor.
Title: Religion in contemporary society / Avery Elizabeth Hurt, book
    editor.
Description: First edition. | New York : Greenhaven Publishing, 2022. |
    Series: Opposing viewpoints | Includes bibliographical references and
    index. | Contents: Religion in contemporary society | Audience: Ages 15+
    | Audience: Grades 10–12 | Summary: "Anthology of diverse viewpoints
that examine religion's place in contemporary society."—Provided
    by publisher.
Identifiers: LCCN 2020050957 | ISBN 9781534507623 (library binding) | ISBN
    9781534507609 (paperback)
Subjects: LCSH: United States—Religion—History—21st century—Textbooks.
    | Religion and sociology—United States—Textbooks.
Classification: LCC BL2525 .R468123 2022 | DDC 200.973—dc23
LC record available at https://lccn.loc.gov/2020050957

Manufactured in the United States of America

Website: http://greenhavenpublishing.com

Contents

Chapter 3: Should Exceptions Be Made for Religious Practices That Are Otherwise Illegal?

Chapter 4: How Do You Define Religion?

The Importance of Opposing Viewpoints

Perhaps every generation experiences a period in time in which the populace seems especially polarized, starkly divided on the important issues of the day and gravitating toward the far ends of the political spectrum and away from a consensus-facilitating middle ground. The world that today's students are growing up in and that they will soon enter into as active and engaged citizens is deeply fragmented in just this way. Issues relating to terrorism, immigration, women's rights, minority rights, race relations, health care, taxation, wealth and poverty, the environment, policing, military intervention, the proper role of government—in some ways, perennial issues that are freshly and uniquely urgent and vital with each new generation—are currently roiling the world.

If we are to foster a knowledgeable, responsible, active, and engaged citizenry among today's youth, we must provide them with the intellectual, interpretive, and critical-thinking tools and experience necessary to make sense of the world around them and of the all-important debates and arguments that inform it. After all, the outcome of these debates will in large measure determine the future course, prospects, and outcomes of the world and its peoples, particularly its youth. If they are to become successful members of society and productive and informed citizens, students need to learn how to evaluate the strengths and weaknesses of someone else's arguments, how to sift fact from opinion and fallacy, and how to test the relative merits and validity of their own opinions against the known facts and the best possible available information. The landmark series Opposing Viewpoints has been providing students with just such critical-thinking skills and exposure to the debates surrounding society's most urgent contemporary issues for many years, and it continues to serve this essential role with undiminished commitment, care, and rigor.

The key to the series's success in achieving its goal of sharpening students' critical-thinking and analytic skills resides in its title—

Opposing Viewpoints. In every intriguing, compelling, and engaging volume of this series, readers are presented with the widest possible spectrum of distinct viewpoints, expert opinions, and informed argumentation and commentary, supplied by some of today's leading academics, thinkers, analysts, politicians, policy makers, economists, activists, change agents, and advocates. Every opinion and argument anthologized here is presented objectively and accorded respect. There is no editorializing in any introductory text or in the arrangement and order of the pieces. No piece is included as a "straw man," an easy ideological target for cheap point-scoring. As wide and inclusive a range of viewpoints as possible is offered, with no privileging of one particular political ideology or cultural perspective over another. It is left to each individual reader to evaluate the relative merits of each argument— as he or she sees it, and with the use of ever-growing critical-thinking skills—and grapple with his or her own assumptions, beliefs, and perspectives to determine how convincing or successful any given argument is and how the reader's own stance on the issue may be modified or altered in response to it.

This process is facilitated and supported by volume, chapter, and selection introductions that provide readers with the essential context they need to begin engaging with the spotlighted issues, with the debates surrounding them, and with their own perhaps shifting or nascent opinions on them. In addition, guided reading and discussion questions encourage readers to determine the authors' point of view and purpose, interrogate and analyze the various arguments and their rhetoric and structure, evaluate the arguments' strengths and weaknesses, test their claims against available facts and evidence, judge the validity of the reasoning, and bring into clearer, sharper focus the reader's own beliefs and conclusions and how they may differ from or align with those in the collection or those of their classmates.

Research has shown that reading comprehension skills improve dramatically when students are provided with compelling, intriguing, and relevant "discussable" texts. The subject matter of these collections could not be more compelling, intriguing, or urgently relevant to today's students and the world they are poised to inherit. The anthologized articles and the reading and discussion questions that are included with them also provide the basis for stimulating, lively, and passionate classroom debates. Students who are compelled to anticipate objections to their own argument and identify the flaws in those of an opponent read more carefully, think more critically, and steep themselves in relevant context, facts, and information more thoroughly. In short, using discussable text of the kind provided by every single volume in the Opposing Viewpoints series encourages close reading, facilitates reading comprehension, fosters research, strengthens critical thinking, and greatly enlivens and energizes classroom discussion and participation. The entire learning process is deepened, extended, and strengthened.

For all of these reasons, Opposing Viewpoints continues to be exactly the right resource at exactly the right time—when we most need to provide readers with the critical-thinking tools and skills that will not only serve them well in school but also in their careers and their daily lives as decision-making family members, community members, and citizens. This series encourages respectful engagement with and analysis of opposing viewpoints and fosters a resulting increase in the strength and rigor of one's own opinions and stances. As such, it helps make readers "future ready," and that readiness will pay rich dividends for the readers themselves, for the citizenry, for our society, and for the world at large.

Introduction

> *"The mythical 'Judeo-Christian tradition' proved an unstable foundation on which to build a common American identity. Today, as American democracy once again grasps for root metaphors with which to confront our country's diversity and its place in the world, the term's recuperation should rightfully alarm us: It has always divided Americans far more than it has united them."*
>
> —"The Problem with the 'Judeo-Christian Tradition,'" by James Loeffler, The Atlantic

It is generally understood that there are two things you should never discuss at dinner: religion and politics. And you should *really* avoid discussing them at the same time! Yet in the modern world, especially in the United States, it can be difficult to avoid either topic—or their overlap.

The two were not intended to overlap. In fact, the US Constitution was deliberately designed to keep them apart. Sectarian violence in Europe was fresh in the memories of the nation's founders; they did not want their new country to be likewise torn apart by religious violence. Though most of them believed in some kind of God, and many were Christian, they designed a government that was agnostic on the issue. God is never mentioned in the US Constitution, and religion is mentioned only in Article VI and in the First Amendment. Article VI forbids any religious test for public office. The First Amendment states that "Congress shall make no law respecting an establishment of religion or prohibiting the free exercise thereof." So, the government can't require someone to belong to a particular religion (or any religion) before they can serve in office. And the government can't promote a religion or interfere with anyone's right to worship as they please, a principle called separation of church and state. And that is that.

Well, not quite. The Constitution seems clear enough, yet the nation has been quibbling about the details of these two passages for most of its 230-plus-year history. Though the nation was not founded on religious principles nor has it ever been officially a religious nation, Americans have always been religious. And so far in the nation's history, the majority of its citizens have been Christian. For this reason, many people believe that the US really is a Christian nation, and many others believe that it should be.

That may be changing, though. In the Western world at least, the number of people who don't belong to any religion and even who don't believe in any god is rapidly increasing. And while the United States is behind in this trend, it seems to be catching up fast. In 1990, less than 10 percent of Americans had no religious affiliation. In 2020, 25 percent owned up to belonging to no particular religion. When charted on a graph, the increase of the non-religious since the early 1990s looks like the profile of a mountain only the intrepid would want to climb.

That's why it's surprising that so much of the current political conversation is concerned—either overtly or more subtly—with religion. Rather than less conversation about religion as the nation becomes increasingly secular, religion seems to be at the back of all debates. Dig into most any current issue and you'll likely find religion in there somewhere. Who should be appointed to the Supreme Court? Should LGBTQ people be allowed to marry? Should religious people be able to discriminate against minorities based on religion? Should religious businesses be forced to serve people of whose lifestyles they disapprove? Is US immigration policy a thinly veiled attempt to keep Muslims out? Those are the questions that this increasingly secular nation finds itself discussing and debating.

The viewpoints in *Opposing Viewpoints: Religion in Contemporary Society* take on these issues and more. In chapters titled "What Are the Limits of Separation of Church and State?" "Do Religious Oaths Outweigh Oaths to the Constitution and Professional Oaths?" "Should Exceptions Be Made for Religious Practices That Are Otherwise Illegal?" and "How Do You Define Religion?," authors explore various aspects of the topic. In many cases, the lines of the debate are not as clearly drawn as you might expect. For example, some argue that laws that were written to protect religious liberty are being used as an excuse to discriminate on the basis of religion. A counter-argument is that the discriminatory aspect of these laws is just a cover for their real purpose: consolidating corporate power.

Other issues are more clear-cut. Should professional health care workers be allowed to refuse care based on their religious beliefs? This seems like an easy one—of course not! They've taken an oath to provide care to anyone who needs it. But the question is not quite so easily settled. When a person believes that the care they're giving actually does more harm than good (say a pain medication that can push a terminal patient over the edge to death or a drug that induces abortion), then caregivers have a moral quandary on their hands.

And what does it mean to be religious anyway? Do all those religiously unaffiliated people lack a belief in God (or a god)? Or do they believe in God but just can't agree on a way to worship that God or whether or not a belief in God even entails worship or adherence to a particular moral code? Can you be religious if you don't believe in God? Can you believe in God and not be religious? And is there a way to respect belief in God without sharing it?

In the coming chapters, you'll find many perspectives that shed light on these issues, and you'll see that the questions are often trickier than they seem at first.

CHAPTER 1

What Are the Limits of Separation of Church and State?

Chapter Preface

The Constitution of the United States has nothing to say about religion—except that the government should stay well out of it, and religion should stay well out of government. Yet what might seem like a very clear intent on the part of the founders has long been the subject of raging debate in the nation ruled by the Constitution they framed.

Most discussions of religion and society in the United States come around to an understanding of the fundamental principle known as the separation of church and state. The importance of this doctrine is not in debate. Exactly what it means, however, is another matter. The doctrine is enshrined in the First Amendment of the Constitution in what is known as "the Establishment Clause." It says that "Congress shall pass no law respecting an establishment of religion."

There is no serious debate that it would violate the Establishment Clause for the government to require people to attend religious services or to provide financial support for churches. That much is clear. However, as the saying goes, the devil (whether you believe in one or not) is in the details. Many people feel strongly that the Establishment Clause prohibits taxpayer funds from being used to support any religious activities or messages. This would prevent church schools from receiving any kind of government aid, for example. Others contend that the government must only be neutral in such matters, not favoring any one religious or private entity over another.

Most Americans take the Establishment Clause and the history of the founding of the nation to clearly demonstrate that the United States does not have an official religion, whatever the implications for law, funding, and Christmas pageants. This means that people are free to worship however they please—or not worship at all—and the government will neither aid these activities (or lack of activities) nor do anything to hinder them. Some Americans, on the other hand, believe that the United States is in fact a "Christian nation" and that the government's laws and policies should reflect this, even in some cases going so far as to limit the number of people of other faiths who can come to live here.

The viewpoints in this chapter approach this complicated issue from a wide range of perspectives. Some see the issue as quite black and white. Others find interesting nuances.

> *"Separation of church and state does not mean a separation of moral reasoning from public policy. Such a goal would be futile."*

Christians Should Respect the Boundaries Between Church and State, but Only to a Point

Neal Hardin

In the following viewpoint, Neal Hardin examines the origin of the principle of separation of church and state, going back to a letter written by Thomas Jefferson in 1802. The author takes a Christian perspective, and this viewpoint is intended to explain to fellow Christians (Baptists, in this case) what, in Hardin's view, the doctrine means, what it doesn't, and how Christians should view it. Neal Hardin is a blogger with a master's degree in theology from the Talbot School of Theology.

"What Does 'Separation of Church and State' Actually Mean?" by Neal Hardin, Ethics and Religious Liberty Commission, August 29, 2019. Reprinted by permission.

As you read, consider the following questions:

1. Why does the author call the phrase *separation of church and state* infamous?

2. What, according to this viewpoint, is "the power of the sword," and how is that key to the division between church and state?

3. How should Christians respond to the boundaries between religion and government, according to the author?

S eparation of Church and State" is one of the most misunderstood phrases is modern political discourse. Yet, it is also a phrase with deep roots in Baptist tradition and one that we, as Christians, should have a healthy understanding of as we seek to engage in the public sphere.

Origins of "Separation of Church and State"

The phrase "separation of Church and State" originates in a letter that our third president, Thomas Jefferson, wrote to the Danbury Baptist Association of Connecticut in 1802. Understanding the background of this letter is key to understanding the meaning of this infamous phrase.

Despite fleeing to the New World to escape religious persecution in Europe and seek religious liberty, many of the settlers of the early colonies did not extend religious freedom to minority religions. During the 17th and 18th centuries, it wasn't uncommon for local governments to levy taxes on citizens to support local clergy. In a society where there were many people of various religious persuasions (mostly Protestant denominations), the question then became, "Whose clergy will be funded through taxation?" In the Congregationalist-dominated Northeast, it was usually a Congregationalist minister. In other parts of the country, the Church of England held sway. Thus, minority denominations such as Baptists and Quakers were left being forced to pay taxes to support religious beliefs that they disagreed with. Many who refused had their property confiscated or were beaten, hanged, or jailed.

Fast-forward to 1801, after the formation of the United States government and the ratification of our Constitution and the First Amendment. Thomas Jefferson had won the election of 1800. The Danbury Baptist Association was worried that the Constitution did not go far enough in protecting religious minorities from the overreaches of government. They wrote a letter to Jefferson, urging that the same mistakes of the past not be made, that "no man ought to suffer in Name, person or effects on account of his religious Opinions—That the legitimate Power of civil Government extends no further than to punish the man who works ill to his neighbour."

Jefferson wrote in response,

> Believing with you that religion is a matter which lies solely between Man & his God, that he owes account to none other for his faith or his worship, that the legitimate powers of government reach actions only, & not opinions, I contemplate with sovereign reverence that act of the whole American people which declared that their legislature should "make no law respecting an establishment of religion, or prohibiting the free exercise thereof," thus building a wall of separation between Church & State.

Jefferson, quoting the First Amendment to the Constitution, sought to reassure the Danbury Baptists that what was written was sufficient to protect their rights and that he was a friend to their cause.

Thus, it's fair to say that Founders like Jefferson meant for some kind of separation between church and state to be present. The government could not establish a state-sponsored religion, but neither could it prohibit others from freely practicing their own religion. However, it's also fair to say that opponents of religion in the 20th and 21st centuries have misused this phrase to try and separate religion from the public sphere far beyond what was originally intended.

What Does the Bible Say?

Scripture also supports the principle of separation of church and state (properly understood). It was these principles which informed early Baptist leaders such as John Leland and Isaac Backus and eventually led to the passage of the First Amendment.

First, separation of church and state means that, at an institutional level, church and government are separate entities. Jesus spoke about this in Matthew 22:21 when he said, "Therefore render to Caesar the things that are Caesar's, and to God the things that are God's," thus making a clear delineation between the "things that are Caesar's" (the government's) and the "things that are God's." Likewise, Jesus spoke of his Kingdom not being of this world (John 18:36) while simultaneously acknowledging through Paul that earthly government is established by God for our good (Rom. 13:1-7). Jesus remains sovereign over both institutions (Matt. 28:18) until such time that he returns to rule and reign in the eschaton (Rev. 11:15). In the meantime, he gives both church and government differing tasks.

The key difference we see between the function of the church and the state comes through the use of the power of the sword. God has given government the power of the sword to punish the wrongdoer in civil matters (Rom. 13:4). The church does not have such authority (Matt. 26:51-56). On the other hand, the church can exercise church discipline in judging matters of doctrine and heresy but not the state (1 Cor. 5:1-13). Thus, there exists a healthy separation of church and state, both institutionally and functionally. This is crucial to the mission of the church, which is the preaching of the gospel. We cannot bring about conversion through the power of the sword vested in the state. Only through the power of God's Spirit can someone be brought unto saving faith in Jesus Christ. "For though we walk in the flesh, we are not waging war according to the flesh. For the weapons of our warfare are not of the flesh but have divine power to destroy strongholds." (2 Cor. 10:3-4)

Practically, this works out much as it is articulated in the First Amendment to the US Constitution. No religious institution is privileged above another, neither is religion privileged above nonreligion. Similarly, the government does not prohibit the free exercise of someone's faith.

What It Doesn't Mean

Though we see that separation of church and state is a valid concept, our modern secular society has come to incorrectly understand this phrase to mean either a separation of morality from lawmaking or a separation of religiously informed opinion from the lawmaker. Both of these are mistaken.

> As people of faith, let us seek to engage the public square in a way which is winsome and accords with God's Word, being mindful of the boundaries which God has established between church and state.

First, separation of church and state does not mean a separation of moral reasoning from public policy. Such a goal would be futile. The process of lawmaking is moral by its very nature. A law is instituted because of an ought. This ought to be done because of such and such, or this ought not to be done. The government's use of coercion would lack any justification without a moral foundation behind the laws which it enforces.

Second, separation of church and state does not mean a separation of religiously informed moral reasoning from public policy. It's often said that religious people who run for office need to check their religion at the door before they make policy. Historically, this would have made no sense to our Founders, most of whom were religious. Philosophically, this also faces issues. Whether secular or religious, everyone brings moral presuppositions to the table. Religious people should not be told to check their beliefs at the door simply because they are religiously based. This smacks of an arrogance which most would not want to be accused of. Everyone, whether religious or secular, should have the freedom to publicly or privately make the case for laws which they believe should be passed.

As Christians, we understand that government ought to be secular in the sense that it does not favor one religion over another. Nor should it favor religion above nonreligion (or vice versa). Yet, a government that seeks to use secular moral reasoning alone will soon find itself adrift amid the sea of ever-changing public opinion. A transcendent moral law is needed which can ground the human and political rights that we cherish today. This is, ultimately, the reason why we allow our political conscience to be properly informed by our faith.

Separation of church and state, properly understood, is a foundational principle which secures the rights and privileges of all citizens under a government and ensures that both government and church function according to their God-given roles. As people of faith, let us seek to engage the public square in a way which is winsome and accords with God's Word, being mindful of the boundaries which God has established between church and state.

> "Americans should be proud that we live in a democracy that welcomes persons of many faiths and none."

The United States Is Not a Christian Nation

Americans United for Separation of Church and State

In the following viewpoint, Americans United for Separation of Church and State takes a close look at what it means to say, as some people do, that America is a "Christian nation." The author examines the Constitution and the founders' views with regard to the role of religion in government and goes on to discuss the history of US court decisions related to religion and the public's views on the matter. Ultimately, the viewpoint argues, Americans should be proud that their government remains neutral and leaves it to individuals to decide what faith, if any, they adhere to. Americans United for Separation of Church and State is a nonpartisan educational and advocacy organization dedicated to advancing the separation of religion and government as the only way to ensure freedom of religion, including the right to believe or not believe, for all.

"Is America a Christian Nation?" Americans United for Separation of Church and State. Reprinted by permission.

As you read, consider the following questions:

1. What would it mean for the nation to be "officially" Christian, according to this viewpoint?
2. Why did the founders of the United States take pains to create a secular government?
3. What sort of language about religion did Jefferson use in the Declaration of Independence, and why did he choose those words, according to the viewpoint?

Is the United States a "Christian nation"? Some Americans think so. Religious Right activists and right-wing television preachers often claim that the United States was founded to be a Christian nation. Even some politicians agree. If the people who make this assertion are merely saying that most Americans are Christians, they might have a point. But those who argue that America is a Christian nation usually mean something more, insisting that the country should be officially Christian. The very character of our country is at stake in the outcome of this debate.

Religious Right groups and their allies insist that the United States was designed to be officially Christian and that our laws should enforce the doctrines of (their version of) Christianity. Is this viewpoint accurate? Is there anything in the Constitution that gives special treatment or preference to Christianity? Did the founders of our government believe this or intend to create a government that gave special recognition to Christianity?

The answer to all of these questions is no. The US Constitution is a wholly secular document. It contains no mention of Christianity or Jesus Christ. In fact, the Constitution refers to religion only twice in the First Amendment, which bars laws "respecting an establishment of religion or prohibiting the free exercise thereof," and in Article VI, which prohibits "religious tests" for public office. Both of these provisions are evidence that the country was not founded as officially Christian.

The Founding Fathers did not create a secular government because they disliked religion. Many were believers themselves. Yet they were well aware of the dangers of church-state union. They had studied and even seen first-hand the difficulties that church-state partnerships spawned in Europe. During the American colonial period, alliances between religion and government produced oppression and tyranny on our own shores.

Many colonies, for example, had provisions limiting public office to "Trinitarian Protestants" and other types of laws designed to prop up the religious sentiments of the politically powerful. Some colonies had officially established churches and taxed all citizens to support them, whether they were members or not. Dissenters faced imprisonment, torture and even death.

These arrangements led to bitterness and sectarian division. Many people began agitating for an end to "religious tests" for public office, tax subsidies for churches and other forms of state endorsement of religion. Those who led this charge were not anti-religion. Indeed, many were members of the clergy and people of deep piety. They argued that true faith did not need or want the support of government.

Respect for religious pluralism gradually became the norm. When Thomas Jefferson wrote the Declaration of Independence, for example, he spoke of "unalienable rights endowed by our Creator." He used generic religious language that all religious groups of the day would respond to, not narrowly Christian language traditionally employed by nations with state churches.

While some of the country's founders believed that the government should espouse Christianity, that viewpoint soon became a losing proposition. In Virginia, Patrick Henry argued in favor of tax support for Christian churches. But Henry and his cohorts were in the minority and lost that battle. Jefferson, James Madison and their allies among the state's religious groups ended Virginia's established church and helped pass the Virginia Statute for Religious Liberty, a 1786 law guaranteeing religious freedom to all.

We the General Assembly of Virginia do enact that no man shall be compelled to frequent or support any religious worship, place, or ministry whatsoever, nor shall be enforced, restrained, molested, or burthened in his body or goods, nor shall otherwise suffer, on account of his religious opinions or belief; but that all men shall be free to profess, and by argument to maintain, their opinions in matters of religion, and that the same shall in no wise diminish, enlarge, or affect their civil capacities.

Jefferson and Madison's viewpoint also carried the day when the Constitution, and later, the Bill of Rights, were written. Had an officially Christian nation been the goal of the founders, that concept would appear in the Constitution. It does not. Instead, our nation's governing document ensures religious freedom for everyone.

Maryland representative Luther Martin said that a handful of delegates to the Constitutional Convention argued for formal recognition of Christianity in the Constitution, insisting that such language was necessary in order to "hold out some distinction between the professors of Christianity and downright infidelity or paganism." But that view was not adopted, and the Constitution gave government no authority over religion. Article VI, which allows persons of all religious viewpoints to hold public office, was adopted by a unanimous vote. Through ratification of the First Amendment, observed Jefferson, the American people built a "wall of separation between church and state."

Some pastors who favored church-state union were outraged and delivered sermons asserting that the United States would not be a successful nation because its Constitution did not give special treatment to Christianity. But many others welcomed the new dawn of freedom and praised the Constitution and the First Amendment as true protectors of liberty.

Early national leaders understood that separation of church and state would be good for all faiths including Christianity. Jefferson rejoiced that Virginia had passed his religious freedom law, noting that it would ensure religious freedom for "the Jew

THOMAS JEFFERSON'S TRUE MEANING IN HIS LETTER TO THE DANBURY BAPTIST ASSOCIATION

Thomas Jefferson's Jan. 1, 1802, letter to the Danbury, Conn., Baptist Association is a seminal document in American church-state history. In the letter, Jefferson used the metaphor of the "wall of separation between church and state," a phrase that, as the Supreme Court once noted, has come to be accepted as an authoritative declaration of the scope and meaning of the First Amendment.

Religious Right groups often spread misinformation about the letter in an attempt to discredit its importance. To set the record straight and understand why the letter is important, it's necessary to read first the Danbury Baptist letter to Jefferson and understand why they sent it.

Religious Right groups frequently assert that the Baptists wrote to Jefferson because they wanted him to issue a proclamation calling for a day of fasting and prayer or because they were alarmed over a rumor they had heard that a national church was about to be established.

These assertions are not true. The Baptists wrote to Jefferson to commend him for his stand in favor of religious liberty and to express their dissatisfaction with the church-state relationship in Connecticut.

Jefferson considered using his reply to explain why he, as president, refused to issue proclamations calling for days of fasting and prayer. Jefferson's attorney general, Levi Lincoln, recommended against this, so Jefferson used the letter to make a statement about the importance of church-state separation.

"History and Origins of Church-State Separation," Americans United for Separation of Church and State.

and the Gentile, the Christian and Mahometan, the Hindoo, the infidel of every denomination."

Other early US leaders echoed that view. President George Washington, in a famous 1790 letter to a Jewish congregation in Newport, R.I., celebrated the fact that Jews had full freedom of worship in America. Noted Washington, "All possess alike liberty of conscience and immunities of citizenship."

Washington's administration even negotiated a treaty with the Muslim rulers of north Africa that stated explicitly that the United States was not founded on Christianity. The pact, known as the Treaty with Tripoli, was approved unanimously by the Senate in 1797, under the administration of John Adams. Article 11 of the treaty states, "[T]he government of the United States is not, in any sense, founded on the Christian religion...."

Admittedly, the US government has not always lived up to its constitutional principles. In the late 19th century especially, officials often promoted a de facto form of Protestantism. Even the US Supreme Court fell victim to this mentality in 1892, with Justice David Brewer declaring in *Holy Trinity v. United States* that America is "a Christian nation."

It should be noted, however, that the *Holy Trinity* decision is a legal anomaly. It has rarely been cited by other courts, and the "Christian nation" declaration appeared in dicta, a legal term meaning writing that reflects a judge's personal opinion, not a mandate of the law. Also, it is unclear exactly what Brewer meant. In a book he wrote in 1905, Brewer pointed out that the United States is Christian in a cultural sense, not a legal one.

A more accurate judicial view of the relationship between religion and government is described by Justice John Paul Stevens in his 1985 *Wallace v. Jaffree* ruling. Commenting on the constitutional right of all Americans to choose their own religious belief, Stevens wrote, "At one time it was thought that this right merely proscribed the preference of one Christian sect over another, but would not require equal respect for the conscience of the infidel, the atheist, or the adherent of a non-Christian faith such as Mohammedism or Judaism. But when the underlying principle has been examined in the crucible of litigation, the Court has unambiguously concluded that the individual freedom of conscience protected by the First Amendment embraces the right to select any religious faith or none at all."

A determined faction of Christians has fought against this wise and time-tested policy throughout our history. In the mid 19th century, several efforts were made to add specific references to Christianity to the Constitution. One group, the National Reform Association (NRA), pushed a "Christian nation" amendment in Congress in 1864. NRA members believed that the Civil War was divine punishment for failing to mention God in the Constitution and saw the amendment as a way to atone for that omission.

The NRA amendment called for "humbly acknowledging Almighty God as the source of all authority and power in civil government, the Lord Jesus Christ as the Ruler among the nations, [and] His revealed will as the supreme law of the land, in order to constitute a Christian government." Ten years later, the House Judiciary Committee voted against its adoption. The committee noted "the dangers which the union between church and state had imposed upon so many nations of the Old World" and said in light of that it was felt "inexpedient to put anything into the Constitution which might be construed to be a reference to any religious creed or doctrine."

Similar theocratic proposals resurfaced in Congress sporadically over the years. As late as 1950, a proposal was introduced in the Senate that would have added language to the Constitution that "devoutly recognizes the Authority and Law of Jesus Christ, Saviour and Ruler of nations, through whom are bestowed the blessings of liberty." This amendment was never voted out of committee. Efforts to revive it in the early 1960s were unsuccessful.

Today, America's religious demographics are changing, and diversity has greatly expanded since our nation's founding. The number of Jews has increased, and more Muslims are living in America than ever before. Other religions now represented in America include Hinduism, Buddhism and a myriad others.

In addition, many Americans say they have no religious faith or identify themselves as atheists, agnostics or Humanists. According to some scholars, over 2,000 distinct religious groups and denominations exist in the United States.

Also, even though most Americans identify as Christian, this does not mean they would back official government recognition of the Christian faith. Christian denominations disagree on points of doctrine, church structure and stands on social issues. Many Christians take a moderate or liberal perspective on church-state relations and oppose efforts to impose religion by government action.

Americans should be proud that we live in a democracy that welcomes persons of many faiths and none. Around the globe, millions of people still dwell under oppressive regimes where religion and government are harshly commingled. (Iran and the former Taliban regime of Afghanistan are just two examples.) Many residents of those countries look to the United States as a beacon of hope and a model for what their own nations might someday become.

Only the principle of church-state separation can protect America's incredible degree of religious freedom. The individual rights and diversity we enjoy cannot be maintained if the government promotes Christianity or if our government takes on the trappings of a "faith-based" state.

The United States, in short, was not founded to be an officially Christian nation or to espouse any official religion. Our government is neutral on religious matters, leaving such decisions to individuals. This democratic and pluralistic system has allowed a broad array of religious groups to grow and flourish and guarantees every individual American the right to determine his or her own spiritual path or to reject religion entirely. As a result of this policy, Americans enjoy more religious freedom than any people in world history. We should be proud of this accomplishment and work to preserve the constitutional principle that made it possible for separation of church and state.

> *"History shows us that only harm comes of uniting church and state."*

America Is a Free Nation

Dan Barker

In the following viewpoint, Dan Barker also argues that America is not a Christian nation. But unlike the previous viewpoint, which looked at the founding documents and history of court rulings, here the author addresses various arguments people often make when defending the idea that America is a Christian nation. Dan Barker is a former evangelical minister, now a freethinker who works with organizations such as the Freedom from Religion Foundation.

As you read, consider the following questions:

1. How does the author define Thomas Jefferson's political beliefs?
2. What is the official United States motto, and how is it used in this viewpoint to support the author's position?
3. What are the limits to majority rule, according to the viewpoint, and why are these important?

"Is America a Christian Nation?" by Dan Barker, Freedom from Religion Foundation. Reprinted by permission.

The US Constitution is a secular document. It begins, "We the people," and contains no mention of "God" or "Christianity." Its only references to religion are exclusionary, such as, "no religious test shall ever be required as a qualification to any office or public trust" (Art. VI), and "Congress shall make no law respecting an establishment of religion, or prohibiting the free exercise thereof" (First Amendment). The presidential oath of office, the only oath detailed in the Constitution, does not contain the phrase "so help me God" or any requirement to swear on a bible (Art. II, Sec. 1). If we are a Christian nation, why doesn't our Constitution say so?

In 1797, America made a treaty with Tripoli, declaring that "the government of the United States is not, in any sense, founded on the Christian religion." This reassurance to Islam was written during Washington's presidency, and approved by the Senate under John Adams.

What About the Declaration of Independence?

We are not governed by the Declaration. Its purpose was to "dissolve the political bands," not to set up a religious nation. Its authority was based on the idea that "governments are instituted among men, deriving their just powers from the consent of the governed," which is contrary to the biblical concept of rule by divine authority. It deals with laws, taxation, representation, war, immigration, and so on, never discussing religion at all.

The references to "Nature's God," "Creator," and "Divine Providence" in the Declaration do not endorse Christianity. Thomas Jefferson, its author, was a Deist, opposed to orthodox Christianity and the supernatural.

What About the Pilgrims and Puritans?

The first colony of English-speaking Europeans was Jamestown, settled in 1609 for trade, not religious freedom. Fewer than half of the 102 *Mayflower* passengers in 1620 were "Pilgrims" seeking religious freedom. The secular United States of America was formed more than a century and a half later. If tradition requires us to return to the views of a few early settlers, why not adopt the polytheistic and natural beliefs of the Native Americans, the true founders of the continent at least 12,000 years earlier?

Most of the religious colonial governments excluded and persecuted those of the "wrong" faith. The framers of our Constitution in 1787 wanted no part of religious intolerance and bloodshed, wisely establishing the first government in history to separate church and state.

Do the Words "Separation of Church and State" Appear in the Constitution?

The phrase, "a wall of separation between church and state," was coined by President Thomas Jefferson in a carefully crafted letter to the Danbury Baptists in 1802, when they had asked him to explain the First Amendment. The Supreme Court, and lower courts, have used Jefferson's phrase repeatedly in major decisions upholding neutrality in matters of religion. The exact words "separation of church and state" do not appear in the Constitution; neither do "separation of powers," "interstate commerce," "right to privacy," and other phrases that have come to represent well-established constitutional principles.

What Does "Separation of Church and State" Mean?

Thomas Jefferson, explaining the phrase to the Danbury Baptists, said "the legitimate powers of government reach actions only, and not opinions." Personal religious views are just that: personal. Our government has no right to promulgate religion or to interfere with private beliefs.

The Supreme Court has forged a three-part "Lemon test" (*Lemon v. Kurtzman*, 1971) to determine if a law is permissible under the First Amendment religion clauses: (1) It must have a secular purpose. (2) It must have a primary effect that neither advances nor inhibits religion. (3) It must avoid excessive entanglement of church and state. The separation of church and state is a precious American principle supported not only by minorities, such as

Jews, Muslims, and unbelievers, but applauded by most Protestant churches that recognize that it has allowed religion to flourish in this nation.

What About Majority Rule?

America is one nation under a Constitution. Although the Constitution sets up a representative democracy, it specifically was amended with the Bill of Rights in 1791 to uphold individual and minority rights. On constitutional matters we do not have majority rule. For example, when the majority in certain localities voted to segregate blacks, this was declared illegal. The majority has no right to tyrannize the minority on matters such as race, gender, or religion.

Not only is it unAmerican for the government to promote religion, it is rude. Whenever a public official uses the office to advance religion, someone is offended. The wisest policy is one of neutrality.

Isn't Removing Religion from Public Places Hostile to Religion?

No one is deprived of worship in America. Tax-exempt churches, temples and mosques abound. The state has no say about private religious beliefs and practices, unless they endanger health or life. Our government represents all of the people, supported by dollars from a plurality of religious and non-religious taxpayers.

Some countries, such as the U.S.S.R., expressed hostility to religion. Others, such as Iran, have welded church and state. America wisely has taken the middle course—neither for nor against religion. Neutrality offends no one, and protects everyone.

The First Amendment Deals with "Congress." Can't States Make Their Own Religious Policies?

Under the "due process" clause of the 14th Amendment (ratified in 1868), the Bill of Rights applies to state citizens. No governor, mayor, sheriff, public school employee, or other public official may violate the human rights embodied in the Constitution. The government at all levels must respect the separation of church and state. Most state constitutions, in fact, contain language that is even stricter than the First Amendment, prohibiting the state from setting up a ministry, using tax dollars to promote religion, or interfering with freedom of conscience.

What About "One Nation Under God" and "In God We Trust"?

The words "under God," did not appear in the Pledge of Allegiance until 1954, when Congress, under McCarthyism, inserted them. Likewise, Congress mandated that "In God We Trust" appear on all currency only in 1955, and it was absent from paper currency prior to 1957. (It appeared on some coins earlier, as did other sundry phrases, such as "Mind Your Business.") "In God We Trust" was belatedly adopted as our national motto in 1956. The official US motto, chosen by John Adams, Benjamin Franklin, and Thomas Jefferson, is *E Pluribus Unum* ("Of Many, One"), celebrating plurality, not theocracy.

Isn't American Law Based on the Ten Commandments?

Not at all! The first four Commandments are religious edicts having nothing to do with law or ethical behavior. Only three—homicide, theft, and perjury—are relevant to modern American law, and these have existed in cultures long pre-dating Moses. If Americans honored the commandment against "coveting," free enterprise would collapse! The Supreme Court has ruled that posting the Ten Commandments in public schools is unconstitutional.

Our secular laws, based on the human principle of "justice for all," provide protection against crimes, and our civil government enforces them through a secular criminal justice system.

Why Be Concerned About the Separation of Church and State?

Ignoring history, law, and fairness, fanatics are working vigorously to turn America into a Christian nation. Right wing Protestants and Catholics would impose their narrow morality on the rest of us, resisting women's rights, freedom for religious minorities and unbelievers, gay and lesbian rights, and civil rights for all. History shows us that only harm comes of uniting church and state.

America has never been a Christian nation. We are a free nation. Anne Gaylor, founder of the Freedom From Religion Foundation, points out: "There can be no religious freedom without the freedom to dissent."

> "*The Founding Fathers clearly
> intended a society of fervent faith,
> freely encouraged by government for
> the benefit of all.*"

The Separation of Church and State Is an Unconstitutional Doctrine

Focus on the Family

In the following viewpoint, Focus on the Family argues that the US Supreme Court has misunderstood and misapplied the doctrine of separation of church and state. The result, the author says, has been to create a hostility toward religion in the United States. While the author agrees that the nation's founders intended to protect the free exercise of religion, he claims that the courts have gone too far and subverted rather than supported the framers' intentions. Focus on the Family is a global fundamentalist Christian ministry that promotes social conservative views on public policy.

As you read, consider the following questions:

1. This author says that the Founding Fathers presupposed America had a Christian identity. How does he justify this claim?
2. In what way, according to this viewpoint, are teacher-led prayers in a classroom different from prayers at a graduation ceremony or a football game? Do you agree?
3. What is the author's proposed solution to the problem of misapplying the doctrine of separation of church and state?

The so-called "wall of separation between church and state" has done more damage to America's religious and moral tradition than any other utterance of the Supreme Court. While the First Amendment was originally intended to prevent the establishment of a national religion and thus ensure religious liberty, the Supreme Court's misuse of the "separation of church and state" phrase has fostered hostility toward, rather than protection of, religious freedom.

This phrase has been used by the Court to outlaw Ten Commandments displays in public buildings, prayer and Bible reading in schools, clergy and even student invocations at school events, and other public acknowledgements of God. Such decisions clearly negate the Founding Father's presupposition of America's Christian identity. It is time to return the First Amendment back to its original meaning and revive the rich faith-filled heritage of America's public life.

National Religion

Many of the state legislatures that ratified the Constitution conditioned their approval on the further inclusion of a guarantee of individual liberties such as the freedom of religion. Some of those states already had taxpayer-supported "establishments" of religion. The new Congress took up these calls for action and drafted the Bill of Rights for further approval by the states. James Madison, a major participant in the debate and drafting of what ultimately became the First Amendment, introduced the initial draft on June 8, 1789 as discussions began in the House:

> The civil rights of none shall be abridged on account of religious belief or worship, nor shall any national religion be established, nor shall the full and equal rights of conscience be in any manner, or on any pretext, infringed.

After further discussion, other versions of the amendment were offered, including: "no religion shall be established by law," "no religious doctrine shall be established by law," "no national religion shall be established by law" and "Congress shall make no laws touching religion." Finally, the House sent back to the Senate this version: "Congress shall make no law establishing religion." The Senate took the House version under advisement, but then offered its own version: "Congress shall make no law establishing articles of faith or a mode of worship, or prohibiting the free exercise of religion." When the House and Senate met to resolve their differing versions, they settled on the ultimate version of "Congress shall make no law respecting an establishment of religion." See generally, *Wallace v. Jaffree*, 472 US 38, 92-98 (1985), Justice Rehnquist, dissenting.

What is clear from the records of the First Amendment debates, as well as Jefferson's own "wall of separation" language, is the Founders' aversion to Congress establishing a national religion, not the religion-scrubbing tool the Supreme Court has made of it over the last 60 years.

A few Supreme Court justices have resisted the current perversion of Jefferson's "wall" metaphor and its effect on the Establishment Clause. In his 1985 dissent from yet another Supreme Court decision invoking Jefferson's "wall" to strike down Alabama's "moment of silence" statute, Chief Justice Rehnquist had this to say:

> It is impossible to build sound constitutional doctrine upon a mistaken understanding of constitutional history, but

unfortunately the Establishment Clause has been expressly freighted with Jefferson's misleading metaphor for nearly 40 years.

In another by-product of the *Everson* decision, the Supreme Court decreed that the First Amendment, which begins "Congress shall make no law…," would henceforth apply to the states as well as the federal government. That's how the Supreme Court gained authority over religious expression in local schoolrooms, graduation ceremonies, football games, courthouses, city councils and thousands of other state and local venues. Although that particular issue is too large to address here, it is further evidence of the Supreme Court's massive power grab in the *Everson* decision.

Values and the Issues at Hand

Focus on the Family affirms the importance of social responsibility, supporting government institutions and protecting them against destructive social influences. God has ordained all social institutions, including the government, for the benefit of mankind and as a reflection of His divine nature. The Supreme Court's imposition of the doctrine of separation of church and state distorts the Founding Father's recognition of our unequivocally Christian nation and the protection of religious freedom for all faiths.

The First Amendment's guarantees were intended as a check on the power of government. They were never intended as a check on religion's influence on the government. Daniel L. Dreisbach, "Origins and Dangers of the 'Wall of Separation' Between Church and State," Imprimis, 35 (2006): p. 5. One of the strengths of our Constitution and the success that we have enjoyed as a country derives from our "unalienable rights" endowed by our Creator. The whole purpose of government is, according to the Declaration of Independence, "to secure these rights." John Adams spoke of the special role that religion and morality play in the successful outworking of the Constitution's provisions: "Our Constitution was made only for a moral and religious people. It is wholly inadequate to the government of any other."

Ironically, the more that courts cleanse the public square of all vestiges of religion and morality, the further we travel from the hope of Jefferson's best work, the Declaration of Independence, and toward his warning that "whenever any form of government becomes destructive of these ends …" change is necessary. We're not advocating a revolution of arms, but of jurisprudence.

What to Do?

We believe that the Establishment Clause was intended to protect religious freedom and that the separation of church and state is an unconstitutional doctrine. We believe that the First Amendment must be restored to its original meaning. We support the reformation of America's courts.

Since the 1947 *Everson* decision, the Court has struggled to formulate and apply various legal tests for governmental actions that cross the line into an unconstitutional "establishment of religion." The only test that makes sense, given the original understanding of the First Amendment's Establishment Clause, is the "coercion test." See generally *Lee v. Weisman*, 505 US 577 (1992). And not just any "coercion test," but the one described by Justice Scalia in his dissent in the 1992 case of *Lee v. Weisman*: coercion by force of law. Scalia's dissent rejected the "psychological coercion" test applied by Justice Kennedy and the liberal majority in that case, which found a clergy invocation at a graduation ceremony (at which participants would supposedly feel some subtle coercion to listen to the words of the prayer rather than leave) unconstitutional. Scalia not only rejected "psychological coercion" as a meaningful term, but went on to explain that using a test of "coercion by force of law" would, for example, prohibit teacher-led prayers during instructional time; but prayers at graduation ceremonies or football games would be permissible.

We think that's a sensible and correct interpretation of the original understanding of the Establishment Clause, and its use would put a stop to the endless Establishment Clause litigation initiated by the ACLU and other liberal organizations against

Christmas displays, city council invocations, student-led prayer and other forms of traditional religious expression.

Focus on the Family also advocates for the appointment of strict constructionist judges who will interpret the Constitution as it was originally understood and who will refrain from re-writing the First Amendment into something it was never intended to be.

Talking Points

- The Founding Fathers intended the First Amendment's Establishment Clause to protect religious freedom in America.
- The Founding Fathers did not intend to establish a wall of separation between church and state.

  · The phrase "wall of separation between church and state" was not even used by the authors of the First Amendment. Instead, the term was used in 1802 by Thomas Jefferson when he argued, in a private letter, that the federal government should not, under the First Amendment, encroach upon religious freedom.

  · The Founding Fathers wrote the First Amendment to prohibit the establishment of a national religion or denomination, not to prohibit public religious expression.

  · Both Washington and Jefferson recommended that government funds be used to support ministries to American Indian tribes, a clear indication that these Founding Fathers recognized no "separation of church and state."

  · A few Supreme Court justices, including Chief Justice William Rehnquist, have recognized that the Court wrongly applied Jefferson's metaphor to the Establishment Clause and unconstitutionally decided that government and religion should remain separate.

- The Founding Fathers clearly intended a society of fervent faith, freely encouraged by government for the benefit of all. They firmly asserted that religion was a general and public concern, the very key to liberty's survival and America's prosperity.
- The federal courts have overstepped the constitutional bounds of judicial power by applying the unconstitutional separation of church and state mantra to religious cases.

  · The Supreme Court extended the First Amendment's religious clauses to state governments as well as Congress, thus increasing the federal courts' authority beyond the Founder's original specification.

  · Instead of separating government and religious spheres, today's courts are dictating rules of religious expression in America, all under the guise of preventing an "establishment of religion."

  · The separation of church and state has fostered hostility toward, rather than protection of, religious freedom, providing false reason to outlaw Ten Commandment displays, prayer and Bible reading in schools, clergy invocation and other religious acknowledgements of God in the public square.

- We believe the First Amendment should be applied as the Founding Fathers originally intended: to protect religious liberties. The rich faith-filled heritage of America's public life must be restored.
- America's courts must be reformed:

  · Activist judges are currently misusing the so-called "wall of separation between church and state" to dictate rules of religious expression and curtail religious freedom in the public square.

· Strict constructionist judges, who view and apply the First Amendment in its original understanding, must be appointed to federal courts.

· Courts must abandon unconstitutional use of the separation of church and state doctrine.

· The Supreme Court's "separation" cases have resulted in the very governmental interference with religion that the First Amendment was designed to prevent.

> "Saying that America is a
> 'predominantly Christian nation'
> would be accurate and not cause
> mischief, as would saying 'America is
> a nation of mostly Christians.'"

The US Supreme Court Did Not Rule That America Is a Christian Nation

Austin Cline

A previous viewpoint referred to the US Supreme Court case Holy Trinity Church v. The United States. *In the following viewpoint, Austin Cline examines that ruling and argues that the justices in that case did not, as some Christians claim, rule that America is a Christian nation. It may be observed to be majority Christian, but that is quite a different matter. Austin Cline is a former director of the Council for Secular Humanism and writes and lectures widely about religion, science, and skepticism.*

"Did the Supreme Court Rule America a Christian Nation?" by Austin Cline, Dotdash Publishing Family, August 4, 2018. Reprinted by permission.

As you read, consider the following questions:

1. What was the *Trinity* case about, and why does the author say that in itself makes it unlikely that the ruling means that the United States is a Christian nation?
2. How did religion even come up in this case, according to the viewpoint?
3. In what sense can the United States be said to be a Christian nation, according to the author?

There are many Christians who sincerely and even vociferously believe that America is a Christian Nation, founded on a belief in and worship of their god. One argument they offer on behalf of this is that the Supreme Court has officially declared America to be a Christian Nation.

Presumably, if America is officially a Christian Nation, then the government would have the authority to privilege, promote, endorse, support, and encourage Christianity—the sorts of things which many of the most radical evangelicals desperately want. Adherents of all other religions, and secular atheists, in particular, would naturally be "second class" citizens.

Holy Trinity

This misunderstanding is based upon the Supreme Court's decision in *Holy Trinity Church v. the United States*, issued in 1892 and written by Justice David Brewer:

> These and many other matters which might be noticed, add a volume of unofficial declarations to the mass of organic utterances that this is a Christian nation.

The case itself involved a federal law which prohibited any company or group to prepay the transportation costs of a non-citizen coming to the United States to work for that company or organization, or indeed even encourage such people from coming here. Obviously, this wasn't a case where religion, religious beliefs, or even just Christianity, in particular, played a big role. It would be very surprising, then, for the ruling to have much at all to say about religion, much less to make a sweeping declaration like "America is a Christian Nation."

Religion became entangled with the issue because the federal law was challenged by Holy Trinity Church, which had contracted with E. Walpole Warren, an Englishman, to come and be a rector for their congregation. In the Supreme Court's decision, Justice Brewer found that the legislation was overly broad because it applied to much more than it should have. He did not, however, base his decision on the idea that, legally and politically, the United States is a "Christian Nation."

Quite the contrary, because the things Brewer lists as indicating that this is a "Christian Nation" he specifically labels as "unofficial declarations." Brewer's point was merely that the people in this country are Christian—thus, it seemed unlikely to him and the other justices that the legislators meant to prohibit churches from inviting famous and prominent religious leaders (even Jewish rabbis) from coming here and serving their congregations.

Perhaps realizing how his phrasing could create mischief and misinterpretation, Justice Brewer published a book in 1905 titled *The United States: A Christian Nation*. In it he wrote:

> But in what sense can [the United States] be called a Christian nation? Not in the sense that Christianity is the established religion or the people are compelled in any manner to support it. On the contrary, the Constitution specifically provides that "congress shall make no law respecting an establishment of religion or prohibiting the free exercise thereof." Neither is it Christian in the sense that all its citizens are either in fact or in name Christians. On the contrary, all religions have free scope within its borders. Numbers of our people profess other religions, and many reject all. [...]
>
> Nor is it Christian in the sense that a profession of Christianity is a condition of holding office or otherwise engaging in public service, or essential to recognition either politically

or socially. In fact, the government as a legal organization is independent of all religions.

Justice Brewer's decision was not, therefore, any attempt to argue that the laws in the United States should enforce Christianity or reflect solely Christian concerns and beliefs. He was simply making an observation which is consistent with the fact that people in this country tend to be Christian—an observation that was certainly even truer when he was writing. What's more, he was forward-thinking enough that he went so far as to deny many of the arguments and claims made by conservative evangelicals down through today.

We could, in fact, paraphrase Justice Brewer's last sentence to say, "Government is and must remain independent of all religions," which strikes me as an excellent way to express the idea of church/state separation.

Saying that America is a "predominantly Christian nation" would be accurate and not cause mischief, as would saying "America is a nation of mostly Christians." This communicates information about what group is a majority without also implicitly conveying the idea that any extra privileges or power should come with being part of the majority.

> *"Is US immigration policy in the Arab region necessary policy or racial animus? ... I think it is a combination of both—but the animus is winning right now."*

There Are Ways to Protect America from Dangerous Extremists Without Discriminating Against Non-Christians

Mohamed 'Arafa

The other viewpoints in this chapter have debated the issue of separation of church and state from a mostly theoretical and historical framework. In the following viewpoint, Mohamed 'Arafa examines a relatively recent example of a presidential executive order that appears to have violated the doctrine upheld by the First Amendment. The author argues that protection from dangerous factions can be achieved without resorting to unconstitutional tactics. Mohamed 'Arafa is a professor of law at Alexandria University in Egypt.

"Donald Trump's Travel Ban: Political, Legal, Moral or Something Else?" by Mohamed 'Arafa, JURIST–Academic Commentary, April 30, 2019. https://www.jurist.org/commentary/2019/04/mohamed-arafa-donald-trumps-travel-ban/
The article was first published by JURIST Legal News & Research Services, Inc. Reprinted by permission.

As you read, consider the following questions:

1. How, according to the author, is the Court's ruling about Trump's travel ban like the Korematsu case that upheld the incarceration of Japanese American citizens during World War II?
2. What evidence does the author offer to support the view that Trump's travel ban was not neutral and was in fact intended to discriminate based on religion?
3. What, according to the viewpoint, was the Court's reasoning in upholding the travel ban, despite evidence that it was aimed at banning people from Muslim countries?

In what may have been one of the most consequential decisions since the notorious *Korematsu* case of 1944, when the Supreme Court upheld the incarceration of Japanese-Americans during World War II, the Court (in June 2018) voted 5-4 to uphold President Donald Trump's travel ban. Like the *Korematsu* judicial ruling, *Trump v. Hawaii* raises questions about procedural formalities while avoiding questions of discrimination and prejudice.

In January 2017, when President Trump's so-called Muslim ban was first declared, it was one of the most alarming executive orders issued by a president in the recent memory. Trump signed a controversial executive order on January 27, 2017, stumbling all refugee admissions and temporarily barring individuals from seven Muslim-majority countries. President Trump's second attempt to bar refugees and immigrants (or even non-immigrants) from several mostly Muslim countries has faced months of legal to-and-fro. The original travel ban included Iraq but an exception was made after it—in the second executive order—was pointed out to the administration that numerous interpreters and others who assisted US troops during the war would have been banned from entering the US also in assisting in fighting radical Islamists and defeating terrorist radical groups like al Qa'daa and Da'esh

(ISIS). And now, the Supreme Court's fresh decision means that individuals from six mainly Muslim nations and refugees will be temporarily banned from the US unless they have a "credible claim of a bona fide relationship with a person or entity" in the country. This offers a main exception to the ban that specialists say will significantly reduce the number of people who can be denied entry. It should be noted that the first version of the travel ban appears to have been envisioned to troll liberals; obviously discriminated based on belief and religion. The very fact of being Muslim was the main reason(s) for inspection and scrutiny. One clause effectively forced a religious test. Thus, refugees facing religious oppression could be admitted but only if "the religion of the individual is a minority religion in the individual's country of nationality."

This revised version, issued in September 2017, seems to be designed to provide legal cover to justify the ban on the other countries that are covered, as Chief Justice John Roberts wrote that the president's order was "neutral on its face." The Supreme Court in *Trump v. Hawaii* held that President Trump's ban on travel from a set of mainly Muslim countries could for now be executed, ignoring reams of evidence that it was motivated by religious animus rather than genuine national security concerns, and the Court's decision doesn't entirely exclude legal challenges to the policy. In holding that the ban could go into effect, though, the Court raised the bar for a successful constitutional test by putting forward a legal norm that is extremely deferential to the government. The Court did not adopt a test often implemented when it's assumed that the government has pursued a religiously discriminatory strategy in violation of the Establishment Clause of the First Amendment of the US Constitution. That test asks the Court to consider whether "a reasonable observer would view the government action as enacted for the purpose of disfavoring a religion." Under the umbrella of the "reasonable observer" test, it is problematic to see how the Court would have permitted the ban to go into effect given the rich record of President Trump's anti-Muslim statements, including those associated with the ban.

Instead, the Court adopted a standard that basically requires claimants to show that animus is the only way to explain the ban.

The president's motive is undoubtedly not neutral in intent. Trump and some of his senior aides have openly expressed animus toward Muslims, Islam, or both. Thus, how much should intent matter? Constitutional law scholars—and the Supreme Court per se—are divided. For instance, Justice Sonia Sotomayor in her dissent cited Trump's rather long paper path to argue that "taking all the relevant evidence together, a reasonable observer would conclude that the Proclamation was driven primarily by anti-Muslim animus." But the extent to which specific inspirations factor more than others is always hard to prove. Further, it's conceivable that someone's intent or motive changes over time. What we do know of the original order is no longer evident in its revised version, so what might have originally been an unambiguously discriminatory "Muslim ban" is something else at the current moment.

Chief Justice John Roberts' majority opinion in favor of the ban draws upon instead on the president's legal authority to block immigration in the name of national security. In this respect, the ruling continues a long tradition of ceding authority over foreign policy to the executive. Yet, the discriminatory origins of the ban do matter. Roberts' opinion focuses on the Immigration and Nationality Act, which gives the US president the power to reject or exclude foreigners if he/she finds that their entry "would be detrimental to the interests of the United States." Yet, to focus entirely on that is treating one of the most discriminatory acts in the modern history of the US as if it was an exercise of presidential power taken by a president acting in conscience.

Roberts' opinion does not entirely ignore Trump's anti-Muslim declarations and its connections to the travel ban. However, he also maintains that the "issue before us is not whether to denounce the statements." Rather, Roberts claims, the court's focus must be on "the significance of those statements in reviewing a presidential directive, neutral on its face, addressing the matter within the core of executive responsibility." That is attorney-speak for saying that, regardless of its clarity, the court is choosing to disregard Trump's anti-Muslim bigotry or racism. Justice Roberts' view is that, the court should accept it at face value no matter what attitudes lie behind it.

That's exactly what the Supreme Court did in the *Korematsu* case. Justice Hugo Black denied that the orders to inter necessitating the custody of Japanese Americans was based on racial bias. The dissenters, particularly Justice Frank Murphy, emphasized that this was outrageous. The Court limited its decision to the validity of the exclusion orders: "the provisions of other orders requiring persons of Japanese ancestry to report to assembly centers and providing for the detention of such persons in assembly and relocation centers were separate, and their validity is not in issue in this proceeding." During the case, the Solicitor General is alleged to have suppressed evidence by keeping from the Court a report from the Office of Naval Intelligence that there was no evidence that Japanese Americans were acting as spies or sending signals to enemy submarines and based on this prosecutorial misconduct.

In the case of the travel ban, Justice Sonia Sotomayor played Murphy's role. Her dissent, joined by Justice Ruth Bader Ginsburg, states that any reasonable observer looking at Trump's record would conclude that the ban was "motivated by anti-Muslim animus." She appeals to the *Korematsu* case in explaining that the government then also evoked national security to justify discriminatory practices. She concluded that "our Constitution demands, and our country deserves, a Judiciary willing to hold the coordinate branches to account when they defy our most sacred legal commitments." In addition to the president's anti-Muslim remarks, the recent complaint offers a substantial amount of public information that destabilizes the administration's story about the policy's genesis. It should be noted that dissenting in *Trump*, Justice Stephen Breyer wrote: "[I]f the Government is not applying the Proclamation's exemption and waiver system, the claim that the Proclamation is a "Muslim ban," rather than a "security-based" ban, becomes much stronger." Legal scholars and political scientists suggest that the waivers from the ban are not being granted to eligible people. Also, the text in the first Muslim ban—a policy functionally equal to the current version—was lifted verbatim from an August 2016 speech then-candidate Trump gave entitled "Understanding the Threat: Radical Islam and the Age of Terror."

Pragmatist Justice Stephen Breyer was joined by Justice Elena Kagan in a thoughtful dissent focused on the system of immunities or exemptions that the executive order authorizes. If those exceptions were to be used, Breyer wrote, it would lend some credibility to the notion that the ban was in fact inspired by national security. The administration's "worldwide review" to recognize insufficiencies in the vetting practices of the world's nearly 200 countries, and inform which to target with travel restrictions, was in fact a mechanism to reverse engineer the original Muslim ban. The current ban substantially overlaps with previous iterations released before the review. However, it excludes people from many countries that meet the review's requirements and permits travel from those that don't. Currently, the government's inclusion in the ban of non-predominantly Muslim countries is a red herring. In practice, very few people will be affected from those countries. Practically, one can imagine that Breyer hopes the travel ban won't really be imposed in practice, and so needs to boost the exemptions to be used. Regrettably, the injustice of the travel ban lies as much in its emblematic (symbolic) outcome as in its barring of individuals from five Muslim-majority countries. This wasn't the right case for Breyer and Kagan to be quite so rational and maybe Breyer also didn't want to alienate Kennedy—the retired justice, succeeded recently by Justice Brett Kavanagh nominated by Trump—whose votes the liberals will need on future matters. Courts may be great places to bend the arc of history toward justice, but they're only great places for that when they agree with whatever we already think is just.

Because the case was before the Supreme Court as the result of a preliminary injunction, not after a trial—according to the general rules within the US procedural legal system—it is still tentatively possible for the lower courts to hold a trial to consider further indication of presidential prejudice. The dilemma is that evidence of Trump's bias has already been acknowledged, realized, and found inadequate by the justices. Hence, without some substantial new piece of evidence, it's complicated to see how a lower court could find that the proclamation was motivated—in real terms—by anti-Muslim bias. To President Trump's supporters, this decision was an affirmation by the highest court in the land of his right to secure United States territorial borders and protect it from terrorism or radical Islamic terrorism, as he always refers to. To opponents, the ruling validated an anti-Muslim agenda that betrayed American values, undermined the Constitution and dashed at the hopes of thousands of families affected by war, persecution, and deprivation. But no deadly terror attacks have been conducted on US soil post-9/11 by any people from the countries on the travel ban list—according to research from the New America Foundation—and none of the perpetrators of the 9/11 attacks were from any of the countries on the travel ban list. Along these lines, critics continue to argue the ban is motivated by anti-Muslim sentiments rather than any real threats to US national security.

The timing of the judgment only reinforced a climate of hostility toward migrants in the West. Three of the Muslim-majority countries affected by Trump's order—Syria, Libya, and Yemen—have known only war for years, while Somalia has suffered through variable degrees of chaos for decades. Though Trump's order ostensibly allows for permits for exemptions on a case-by-case basis. The administration has argued that courts have no role to play because the president has broad powers over immigration and national security, and foreigners have no right to enter the country. Legal scholars have said in written arguments that Trump's September proclamation laying out the current policy comports with immigration law and does not violate the Constitution because it does not single out Muslims. The challengers have said that Trump is flouting immigration law by trying to keep more than 150 million individuals, most of them Muslim, from entering the country. They also argue that his policy amounts to the Muslim ban that he called for as a candidate, violating the Constitution's prohibition against religious bias.

The practical effects on the two non-Muslim majority nations covered by the travel ban—Venezuela and North Korea—are negotiable. The limitations on Venezuelans apply only to a narrow group of public officials. North Koreans for their part, have never been allowed to travel outside their country by their own repressive government. "Most people have forgotten that North Korea was added to the list of countries subject to the ban, mostly as a way of making it look less like an anti-Muslim measure," according to Evans J.R. Revere, a former State Department diplomat who is an expert on North Korea. Also, Sung-Yoon Lee, a professor of Korean studies at Tufts University, said, "The inclusion of North Korea is likely to be reversed by the administration—that is, used as a chip in further advancing the illusion of rapprochement."

Iranians are especially affected by the ban. Approximately one million American citizens of Iranian origin live in the United States. Jamal Abdi, Vice President of Policy at the National Iranian American Council, a Washington-based advocacy group, said that "Iranians cannot travel here [US] unless they get a waiver. The waiver process is unpredictable, with no explanation of how it will be implemented." The impact of the ban, as well as Trump's decision to withdraw from the 2015 nuclear deal with *Korematsu* and *Trump vs. Hawaii* are both cases where the Supreme Court relinquished its moral leadership.

Trump's opinions are obnoxious and hateful to logic and human experience. Trump's speeches, declarations, and comments cannot be elapsed or ignored and perhaps now is as good a time as any for the current President to absorb the age-old concept that a person's uncontrolled statements can come back to haunt them. The debate over the Trump White House's attitude toward Muslims is more than merely academic. Previous presidents have gone out of their way to say their problems are not with Islam as a faith, if only to serve as a public counterbalance to their use of US military power in or against Muslim nations. "The face of terror is not the true faith of Islam," President George W. Bush said shortly after the 9/11 attacks, "that's not what Islam is all about. Islam is peace." President Obama has made comparable remarks, noting that "it's very important for us to align ourselves with the 99.9% of Muslims who are looking for the same thing we're looking for, order, peace, prosperity." There's an old saying, "one bad apple spoils the bunch."

This holds true when we discuss both the historical and current general perspective of Americans or Westerns towards Arabs and Muslims. Why have I stated Arabs and Muslim throughout this essay? They are separate and diverse peoples. Not every Arab is a Muslim and not every Muslim is an Arab. What have we seen by tracking US immigration policy throughout history? We have seen that the general attitudes of the US towards non-white, non-Christian people to be extremely negative and highly deserving of the word "animus." US courts of the past adopted and supported these same points of view. Animus against Arabs and Muslims was very obvious in the opinions of US courts who classified them among the "undesirables." The US must accept some of the blame for allowing these radical groups to promulgate and commit the terrorist acts against humanity which have stricken so much fear and distrust into western society. Is US immigration policy in the Arab region necessary policy or racial animus?

I think it is a combination of both—but the animus is winning right now. The "extreme" tactics and rhetoric promulgated by President Trump and his supporters is a complete showing of animus guised in the veil of legitimate policy. However, given that these groups do exist and that they are a real threat to all persons—not just westerners—legitimate, intelligent policies must be in play to minimize the damage they cause until humanity learns to live with itself peacefully. These policies must be consistent across all races, faiths, and classes of immigrant. The "extreme vetting" of persons from certain states only serves the message of extremists—the US is a racist beast that disdains all non-white, non-Christians. The US is a beautiful place to live with so much promise. When American or westerns call themselves the "Melting Pot," they must ask if they mean this sincerely or not. Do they really welcome all faiths and races or only those that conform to their certain points of view? In other words, must one assimilate to be part of the melting pot or will they forget animus of the past? I hope so. The world is a much more beautiful place when there is a plethora of colors, shapes, ideas, beliefs, and points of views.

Periodical and Internet Sources Bibliography

The following articles have been selected to supplement the diverse views presented in this chapter.

Emile Doak, "You Can't Separate Politics and Theology," *The American Conservative*, September 10, 2019. https://www
.theamericanconservative.com/articles/what-sohrab-ahmari-got
-right/

Garrett Epps, "Constitutional Myth #4: The Constitution Doesn't Separate Church and State," *Atlantic*, June 15, 2011. https://www
.theatlantic.com/national/archive/2011/06/constitutional-myth
-4-the-constitution-doesnt-separate-church-and-state/240481/

Linda Greenhouse, "Let's Not Forget the Establishment Clause," *New York Times*, May 23, 2019. https://www.nytimes.com/2019/05/23
/opinion/abortion-supreme-court-religion.html

Thomas Jefferson, "Letter to the Danbury Baptists," January 1, 1802, US Library of Congress. https://www.loc.gov/loc/lcib/9806
/danpre.html

James Lankford and Russell Moore, "The Real Meaning of the Separation of Church and State," *Time*, updated January 16, 2018. https://time.com/5103677/church-state-separation-religious
-freedom/

Sara Miller Llana, "In Separation of Church and State, Which Institution Is Being Protected? *Christian Science Monitor*, January 14, 2020. https://www.csmonitor.com/World
/Americas/2020/0114/In-separation-of-church-and-state
-which-institution-is-being-protected

Luis Miguel, "Supreme Court Upholds State Funding for Montana Religious Schools," *New American*, June 30, 2020. https://www
.thenewamerican.com/culture/education/item/36209-supreme
-court-upholds-state-funding-for-montana-religious-schools

James R. Rogers, "Incorporating the Establishment Clause, Wrongly," Law and Liberty, November 29, 2019. https://lawliberty.org
/incorporating-the-establishment-clause-wrongly/

Hana M. Ryman and J. Mark Alcorn, "Establishment Clause (Separation of Church and State)," *The First Amendment Encyclopedia*, originally published 2009. https://www.mtsu.edu/first-amendment/article/885/establishment-clause-separation-of-church-and-state

Valerie Strauss, "How the Supreme Court's Decision on Religious Schools Just Eroded the Separation Between Church and State," *Washington Post*, June 30, 2020. https://www.washingtonpost.com/education/2020/06/30/how-supreme-courts-decision-religious-schools-just-eroded-separation-between-church-state/

Nelson Tebbe, Micah Schwartzman, and Richard Schragger, "The Quiet Demise of the Separation of Church and State," *New York Times*, June 8, 2020. https://www.nytimes.com/2020/06/08/opinion/us-constitution-church-state.html

Ed Whelan, "This Day in Liberal Judicial Activism—February 10," National Review, February 10, 2020. https://www.nationalreview.com/bench-memos/this-day-in-liberal-judicial-activism-february-10-2/

CHAPTER 2

Do Religious Oaths Outweigh Oaths to the Constitution and Professional Oaths?

Chapter Preface

I n the previous chapter, viewpoint authors discussed the theory and practice of separation of church and state. The following chapter's viewpoint authors turn their attention to specific situations in which that principle is tested, namely when ministers preach politics from the pulpit and when health care workers refuse care to patients because of their own religious convictions.

Health care workers often find themselves in morally, and sometimes legally, precarious positions. If they are strongly opposed to certain actions—take abortion as an example—they may feel that it is their responsibility to refuse to take part in that action in any way. Yet they have taken an oath to care without fear or favor of anyone who needs their care. If the care is legal, then they are quite likely violating law to refuse care. If they don't refuse care, they may feel that they have violated their faith. As you will see in the coming viewpoints, this problem affects pharmacists as well as physicians, nurses, and emergency medical personnel.

Until recently, churches have been, for the most part, disinclined to get involved in political matters. The pulpit was for sharing God's word, not campaigning for candidates. But more and more ministers, particularly evangelical preachers, are stepping into the political debate and not only urging their followers to support specific issues, such as the anti-abortion movement or opposition to LGBTQ rights, but in violation of federal law, they often endorse or oppose individual candidates. Several of the viewpoints in this chapter deal with that issue. The first gives an overview of the problem and features comments from voices on both sides of the issue.

> *"On Sunday, 33 ministers will take part in a nationwide effort to violate the 54-year-old ban on political preaching and endorse or oppose a candidate from the pulpit."*

The US Government's Regulation of Religious Sermons Is Unconstitutional

Barbara Bradley Hagerty

Federal law prohibits any organization that has tax-exempt status from endorsing or opposing political candidates. In the following viewpoint, Barbara Bradley Hagerty explains some of the complexities of that prohibition and ways in which many pastors are responding to it, participating in an event known as the Pulpit Initiative. As ministers push to challenge the law, will the US government (via the IRS) become more involved in religion? An alliance of pastors hopes the US Supreme Court will find the government's regulation of sermons unconstitutional. Barbara Bradley Hagerty is an American journalist and author.

As you read, consider the following questions:

1. Why did Reverend Booth send to the IRS an article about his sermon that violated the ban on political endorsements by tax exempt organizations?
2. What is the rationale, as explained by Celia Roady, for denying tax exemption to churches that endorse or oppose political positions or candidates?
3. What is Eric Williams's argument against endorsing candidates from the pulpit?

On Sunday, more than 30 pastors across the country are expected to preach a sermon that endorses or opposes a political candidate by name. This would be a flagrant violation of a law that bans tax-exempt organizations from involvement in political campaigns.

Among the pastors expected to violate the ban is Pastor Gus Booth.

Booth will endorse Republican nominee John McCain—four months after delivering a sermon opposing the two main candidates seeking the Democratic presidential nomination.

In May, Booth told his 150 congregants of the Warroad Community Church in Warroad, Minn., that the next president will determine policy on issues like same-sex marriage and abortion.

"If you're a Christian, you cannot support a candidate like Barack Obama or Hillary Clinton," Booth said.

With that, Booth gleefully zipped by the line barring ministers from engaging in political campaigns. The IRS bars people from endorsing or opposing specific candidates from the pulpit. Booth sent an article about his sermon to the IRS so the agency wouldn't miss it. He and his elders knew he would be jeopardizing the church's tax-exempt status.

But, he says, it's his job to evaluate candidates in light of biblical teachings.

"Bottom line is, I'm a spiritual leader in this community, and spiritual leaders need to make decisions. We need to lead spiritually, and we need to be able to speak about the moral issues of the day. And right now, the moral issues of today are also the political issues of today," he said.

The Pulpit Initiative

On Sunday, 33 ministers will take part in a nationwide effort to violate the 54-year-old ban on political preaching and endorse or oppose a candidate from the pulpit. The effort is called the Pulpit Initiative.

Two weeks ago, more than 100 pastors squeezed into a hotel meeting room in Washington, D.C., to learn about the Pulpit Initiative, a brain child of the conservative legal group Alliance Defense Fund. Attorney Erik Stanley walked them through it.

"If the IRS chooses to come after these churches, we will sue the IRS in federal court," Stanley said.

Stanley says pastors are fed up. In the past four years, the IRS has stepped up its investigations of clergy. It sent letters to 47 churches, including some liberal ones—not just for explicit endorsements, but also for using code words like pro-choice or pro-life in relation to candidates.

"What's been happening is that the government has been able to go into the pulpits of America, look over the pastor's shoulder, and parse the content of their sermon. And that's unconstitutional," Stanley said. "No government official should entangle itself with religion in that way."

Stanley says the pastors will try to take their challenge all the way to the US Supreme Court, hoping that the current conservative-leaning composition of the court, headed by Chief Justice John Roberts, will strike down the ban. He says the law infringes on the religious speech of ministers.

Celia Roady disagrees. Roady, a lawyer and expert on charities law, says there's nothing to stop pastors from talking about issues in light of scripture. But, she says, "You simply cannot say to your congregation, you should not vote for Candidate X because of Candidate X's position on this one issue. That's simply the line that has been drawn."

Roady says if a church can endorse a candidate, it is using tax-free dollars—taxpayer money—to subsidize a political campaign.

But it's not merely tax deductions that are at stake here, says Ohio Pastor Eric Williams. He says it's also the attempt of some churches to move aggressively into politics.

"I ask myself, 'Hmm. Why would a religious leader want to oppose a candidate? Why would a religious leader want to stand up and ask for my support for a candidate who's running for office?' They want to gain influence in the governmental process," Williams said.

Williams is senior minister of North Congregational United Church of Christ in Columbus. He says he's seen this before. Two years ago, he reported two conservative megachurches for allegedly endorsing a Republican candidate for governor. The IRS investigated one of the churches. Williams is also concerned that pastors in swing states like Ohio, Pennsylvania and Virginia will be telling their congregants how to vote.

"My concern is that an extreme segment of the Christian faith today is seeking to establish themselves as the public religion of our nation," Williams said.

Williams and some other ministers have filed a formal complaint with the IRS about the Pulpit Initiative. Several tax attorneys said they believe the churches will ultimately lose. They point out that in 1983, the Supreme Court upheld a ban on political endorsements by charities.

So what will happen if Booth's church in Minnesota loses its tax-exempt status?

"Big deal," he said. He added that he can get it back the next day because churches are automatically tax-exempt.

Besides, he said, electing "Godly people is more important than money."

> "To parachute political talking points
> into the text is spiritual malpractice."

Ministers Should Not Preach Politics from the Pulpit

Daniel Darling

In the previous viewpoint, several ministers shared their reasons for violating the legal ban on endorsing candidates from the pulpit and advising parishioners what positions they should take on current issues. In the following viewpoint, Daniel Darling argues that ministers must stick to the scripture and avoid preaching politics from the pulpit. The author gives three reasons to support his argument. Daniel Darling is a protestant minister, author, and blogger.

As you read, consider the following questions:

1. What does the author mean by writing that the Bible is not partisan?
2. In what situations does the viewpoint support pastors speaking from the pulpit about contemporary issues?
3. What is the author advising when he says that pastors should "winsomely engage the culture"?

"Three Reasons Not to Preach Politics in the Pulpit," by Daniel Darling, October 21, 2012. Reprinted with permission by Daniel Darling.

To preach is a humble and holy task. Church attenders arrive with the assumption that what is said comes from the Bible. To cut and paste partisan talking-points or to substitute consistent exegesis with sample "election season" sermons is spiritual malpractice.

Here are three important reasons why pastors shouldn't preach politics in the pulpit:

1. Our Text Must Be the Word of God

This sounds like a cliche, but it bears saying: faithful Bible preachers use the text of the Word of God as their source of preaching. Anything less is simply a speech, which may be inspirational, moral, or even Christian-themed. But if our basis is not the text, we're not preaching.

Sometimes a given text will make political or moral statements. For instance, if you're preaching through Psalm 139, you cannot escape the references to the sanctity of life. Or if you are preaching through Proverbs you will encounter many economic truths that shape capitalism. Or if you are preaching through parts of James or Timothy, you will find it inescapable to avoid the harsh condemnations of greed.

But as a rule pastors, especially those who preach in an expository (taking a book at a time, chapter at a time, verse at a time) approach, will be guided by the text. To parachute political talking points into the text is spiritual malpractice.

One caveat is this: perhaps a pastor will do a topical series on key issues of the day and how Christians should think through them biblically. I've done this as a Sunday Night series. This can be helpful, however, a pastor must be faithful to let the text speak to the issue and not wedge your particular political opinion into the text.

2. The Bible Cuts Both Ways

I find it fascinating that certain groups on the Right want pastors to "speak up." What they mean by this, of course, is to more overtly endorse their preferred candidates and/or moral issues. But what they don't understand is that pastors are speaking up, it's just that what pastors are speaking up about may not be the talking points of the current season. And, the Bible cuts against both parties, against all political persuasions. Yes, there is much in the Scripture affirming the prolife (Psalm 139; Genesis 2-3) and traditional marriage (Mark 19:5) positions. You can also make a good argument that the Bible affirms the idea of limited government (1 Timothy 2:2; Mark 12:17) and some of the root ideas of capitalism. So some would say the Bible is very conservative. And yet that would be incomplete, because you will also find in Scripture many texts on justice, the plight of the poor, treatment of the immigrant. And who Jesus' chief antagonists were in the gospels? The Pharisees, the Religious Right of their day.

Should pastors speak about in the pulpit about contemporary issues? Yes, but only when the texts of Scripture clearly articulate it. They shouldn't bow to any party's talking points. They shouldn't slant their sermons to fit a political profile. They shouldn't become wannabee pundits in the pulpit. They should preach the Word and let it do its work in the hearts of the people, who will then go influence their communities.

3. We Must Never Dilute the Message of the Gospel

The Church should be counter-cultural and should engage the issues of the day. But this engagement should be an outgrowth of the gospel's sanctifying work in each believer. In other words, the political issues shouldn't be the main thing that characterizes a church. The gospel should be the main thing. The Scriptures should be the main thing. Christ should be the main thing. This is why pastors often shy away from endorsements or public pulpit activism. It sends the wrong message that the main purpose for gathering on Sunday is to stir up the troops and get "our guy" elected. But what of the brother or sister of the other party or the soul seeking God who only hears partisan talking points? If this happens, we've failed in our mission.

To be clear, pastors are citizens, too. And so in other venues, such as op-eds, blogs, books and other places of influence the pastor may speak his mind. Even so, he must jealously guard that influence and always speak winsomely. Again, as a minister of the gospel, he must not make politics more important than his pastoral duties.

Pastors should also coach their members to winsomely engage the culture. We need gospel preachers at all levels of society and in all spheres, politics included. Pastors should equip, encourage, and support those who enter public service.

Summary: In conversations I've had and in my own experience, it is mission that keeps pastors from overtly preaching politics in the pulpit and not the IRS.

> *"Open, peaceful societies are inclusive societies; they embrace everyone. And that is likewise the calling of religious leaders: to reach out to all."*

All Kinds of Religious Leaders Are Essential for Building Peaceful Societies

Justin Welby

In the previous viewpoint, we heard from a Protestant minister on why preachers should keep politics out of the pulpit. He said, however, that there are many places in the Bible that support parts of the conservative agenda (at least as that agenda is pursued in the United States). In the following viewpoint, Justin Welby introduces and then includes a speech by Canon Sarah Snyder, founder of Rose Castle Foundation, an international center for reconciliation and peace building. In the speech, Snyder, a citizen of the UK, argues that religious leaders can play a crucial role in building peaceful societies. Justin Welby is Archbishop of Canterbury.

Canon Sarah Snyder, Rose Castle Foundation, "Why All Kinds of Religious Leaders Are Essential for Building Peaceful Societies," Justin Welby, October 20, 2016. Reprinted by permission.

As you read, consider the following questions:

1. How can religious leaders avoid being used by politicians, according to the viewpoint?
2. Much of the political debate in the West these days involves how to deal with the threat from extremist factions, mostly, but not exclusively, in the Middle East. How does Snyder suggest dealing with this problem?
3. How do you think the author of the previous viewpoint, Daniel Darling, would respond to this speech?

In her speech Dr. Snyder emphasised the importance of working with local leaders of religious communities—men, women and young people (including lay leaders). She highlighted the crucial role of women as active peace-builders, and the widespread authority, access and action of religious leaders, who can access vast percentages of populations in countries affected by conflict and extremism.

Dr. Snyder was speaking in a panel debate entitled, "How can open and plural societies help in peace-building? Why do we see extremist groups emerge in failed states?"

Read the speech:

It is an honour to be here today, and to see so many familiar faces from around the globe already pushing the frontiers of peace-building in challenging circumstances. Faith leaders play a vital role, every single day, in promoting and modelling the protection and dignity of all—to honour, forgive, respect and love the "other" in the midst of violence and despair. Jesus calls us to love our enemies and pray for those who persecute us (Matt 5:44)—and as we know too well, that is an almost impossible task, humanly speaking.

But I bring you an example of hope from our very own Archbishop, and his third meeting with Pope Francis last month. Their growing friendship marks a historic moment for ecumenical relations, and a genuine opportunity for collaboration between the

Anglican Communion and the Roman Catholic Church. Such a moment was unthinkable for many of us, even a generation ago. We have journeyed a long way in the last 50 years!

We sometimes forget here in the West that many of the states troubled by violent extremism are deeply religious societies. Religion is not an optional extra, or one dimension among many—it infuses every aspect of life, including the political. The co-operation of religious leaders is vital to the building of inclusive, plural—and peaceful—societies. While religion is rarely the foundational cause of violence, our sacred texts and traditions can be, and are, hijacked to promote extremist agendas. Religion—all religions—must be recognised overwhelmingly as a source of peace, not violence. And religious leaders play a critical role in drawing their communities back to these foundational principles.

Of course, "religious leaders" are not a homogeneous group. In religion, as in politics, leaders have too often abused their power to further corruption, pernicious ideologies and even violence. Mercifully, such leaders are a small minority, and in any case I am not here to exalt the moral rectitude of religious leaders. Rather I want to show you how religious leaders occupy a unique position in their societies which, in my experience, can be pivotal to bringing lasting openness and peace.

First of all, in much of today's world, religious leaders have authority across large percentages of the population. As faith leaders, they speak to the heart of people's decision-making and identities. It is they who set the parameters of acceptable behaviour, who can initiate the transition from conflict to cooperation.

Committing acts of violence towards a fellow human being requires de-facing the other, erasing their humanity and identity. Reconciliation is the process of re-humanising the other. Faith leaders have the authority and means to give communities in conflict the permission to do just that. In Egypt, for example, Bishop Mouneer and his diocese are running the Imam-Priest Exchange. This initiative brings together Muslim and Christian leaders, so they can meet face-to-face, modelling the same for their local communities. If we try to effect societal change without involving religious leaders, we are ignoring some of the most important catalysts for that process.

Of course, when including religious leaders at the peace-building tables, it is important to recognise the role they play straddling all dimensions of life, not just a small portion termed "religious." It is equally important not to undermine the very authority which gives them influence and credibility. The beliefs and priorities which religious leaders hold must be heard and recognised. When this happens, and it is beginning to happen, these leaders are empowered as agents of change, not instrumentalised by politicians but motivated to act with conscience. In January of this year, I had the privilege of witnessing Muslim leaders lead the way in defending the rights of religious minorities at the landmark Marrakesh Declaration. Drawing on the earliest Islamic principles of the Medina Charter, this initiative recognises the responsibility to protect minority communities in Muslim-majority contexts. The challenge now is to move this through to action...

When I talk about religious leaders, I am not just talking about clergy, imams, rabbis, monks and the like. I am talking about the leaders of religious communities at every level, including men, women and youth. Although we work with the symbolic national and international figure-heads, who provide visible leadership for thousands, sometimes millions, we should not underestimate the extraordinary impact of local leaders—both religious and lay. Religious communities are listening to their leaders week in, week out, whether speaking from the pulpit or in their day-to-day interactions. These leaders are widely known, and hold positions of respect and authority in their community—their influence on attitudes and behaviour can be a profound motivator for non-violence.

And this points to a second important reality: religious leaders not only have authority, they have access. This is crucial. If violent extremism is to be tackled effectively, it must be challenged on all fronts. Religious leaders have access to all ages and all social strata. This is something the Archbishop saw first-hand when he visited each of the Anglican provinces around the world. Faith communities have deep roots, permeating societies in a way that—in most countries—state apparatus simply cannot.

Open, peaceful societies are inclusive societies; they embrace everyone. And that is likewise the calling of religious leaders: to reach out to all. In 2013 the Archbishop visited Mexico, travelling with Bishop Francisco Moreno to a village in the Bishop's own diocese of Northern Mexico. This was a challenging region where leaders rarely visited, but where an Anglican priest had worked with the community to provide access to education and employment. It was an area beyond state reach, inaccessible but for the presence of the Church.

As this example in Mexico illustrates, the presence of faith communities spreads far beyond places of worship. Across the Anglican Communion, Anglican schools play a very important political and societal role. A large proportion of Pakistan's current political elite were educated in Anglican schools. The same is true in Sri Lanka where Trinity College in Kandy produces many of that nation's Members of Parliament. By working with faith leaders you are accessing both the educational systems which nurture the future political class, and the grassroots communities in which open, peaceful societies are made or broken.

The access of religious leaders not only crosses socioeconomic barriers but extends to both genders. As you will know, peace-building without women is impossible, and women are usually on the front-line of peace-building in their communities. Time and again it has been demonstrated that women are the "early warning system" for violence, spotting shifts in attitude and behaviour far ahead of trends picked up externally.

Open, plural societies cannot exist without the active participation and flourishing of women. Faith communities at the grassroots level are largely driven by the efforts of women—and in the Anglican Church they are playing key roles at the highest levels. One of the largest women's network in the world is a Christian organisation—the Mothers' Union, with four million members. Both the Anglican Communion and the Mothers Union operate on the same provincial, diocesan and parish system which gives them far-reaching access.

The Mothers' Union are leading the way in enabling women to move from being the victims of violence to active agents of conflict transformation. In Burundi and the Democratic Republic of Congo, for instance, members are working to challenge gender-based violence. They run local advocacy initiatives and also contributed to the "Ending Sexual Violence in Conflict" summit held here in London two years ago.

So working with religious leaders is imperative because of their authority and their access and, finally, because of their action on the ground. As Christians, we start with Jesus Christ, who said: "Blessed are the peacemakers for they shall be called the children of God." Reconciliation with God is what Jesus offers to us through Himself, that we might be reconciled with one another. Reconciliation is at the heart of our faith, and has been at the heart of the Church's work for a very long time.

Two weeks ago we were celebrating the faithful life of nonviolence of St. Francis of Assisi, whose meeting with the Sultan Malik al-Kamil is an early example of a peaceful Christian-Muslim encounter. In more recent history, we can look to the reconciliation ministry of Coventry Cathedral which was devastated by bombing in the Second World War, and reached out in reconciliation instead of retaliation. Since then, Coventry has gone on to promote reconciliation work globally with an ever-growing Community of the Cross of Nails bringing together people and institutions of peace worldwide, from Germany to Burundi.

In the Roman Catholic Church, the Community of Sant'Egidio has worked throughout Mozambique for many years and played a leading role in the negotiations which brought peace there in 1992. In northern Nigeria, the Emir of Kano is bringing to fruition a project which is likely to benefit around a million farmers, thus depriving extremist groups of their foot soldiers. I could go on.

What I hope this shows is that religious leaders are already working in so many different contexts both to prevent violent extremism and to re-build trust in the wake of conflict.

This is because people of faith, and those who lead them, are living in the midst of conflict. For them, peace and violence are not abstract concepts—they are daily realities. The largest single Mothers' Union group in the world is in Baghdad, where over 3000 members have been working for years to build hope and stability in communities continually under threat. So many of our bishops, including Archbishop Ben, have spent their lives walking in the midst of conflict, seeking to understand its drivers and transformative potential. When you work with faith leaders, you engage the people with first-hand experience to resource and enact peaceful transformation.

Many faith communities across the world are modelling openness, inclusivity and peace every day. We have ample opportunity to build on that work so that not only communities but whole societies become open, inclusive and peaceful places where violent extremism is given less oxygen.

Religious leaders have the authority to speak into existing conflicts and divisions. Through their presence, they have unrivalled access across boundaries of age, gender, geography, education. And they have the capacity and vocation for action. To engage with religious leaders, of course, requires theological and cultural sensitivity. But the possibilities when we do so are transformative and offer authentic hope.

"Removing religion from political discourse doesn't remove morality or value-based decision-making."

Religion Shouldn't Have a Place in Political Decisions

Sam Killermann

In the following viewpoint, Sam Killermann agrees with the author of the second viewpoint in this chapter. Religion shouldn't have a place in politics, he argues. But his take is different from all of the previous viewpoints. Killermann contends that political positions should be argued on merits that stand on their own without the need to rely on religious doctrines or dogma. Sam Killermann is an activist, artist, and author who creates tools for global justice.

As you read, consider the following questions:

1. What do you think the author means when he says that it's impossible to have true separation of church and state?
2. How can arguments based on religion add to polarization, according to the viewpoint?
3. What, according to the author, will removing religion from political arguments *not* do?

"I'm Not Anti-Christian, but Religion Shouldn't Have a Place in Political Decisions," by Sam Killermann, It's Pronounced Metrosexual.

L et's make a deal. Promise me that you'll do everything in your power to read this entire article (all 800 words of it) before you start mentally formulating the comment/email/death threat you're going to respond with.

If you can make that promise, read on. If not, go find a website that reinforces your current dispositions on the matter and read that instead. We'll both be happier for it.

In a society where most people (politicians in particular) have some sort of faith that guides their decisions, it's impossible to have a true separation of church and state. That's fine. I don't think we need to only elect atheistic representatives. In fact, I'm candidly against that idea.

What I am suggesting is we create and support a system where political decisions are made based on arguments that stand on their own merits without a religious crutch. Or, to put it another way, "the Bible tells me so" is off limits as an argument. But that doesn't mean what you're arguing for will have to change. All it means is people need to use objective, measurable evidence to defend their arguments, instead of just referring to their faith and leaving it at that.

If something is bad, or will lead to a lower quality of life for folks, or—God forbid—a "moral landslide," explain to me why. And do it without a single reference to dogma.

Why Is This Important?

Because not everyone shares your faith, and it's a politician's responsibility to represent their constituents. Arguments made solely based on a particular faith don't mean much to people who don't share that faith. They do, however, serve as a great catalyst to polarize arguments and create two groups that have no common language, are unable to actually discuss a problem, and just generally hate each other (e.g., pro-choice people vs. anti-choice people in the abortion debate).

It's important because conversation is a necessary component for discussion and democracy, and you can't have a conversation with someone if you don't speak the same language.

How Might the Alternative Work?

As an example, a commonly-argued, religiously-slanted issue is marriage equality (and one you don't have to guess my bias on). Right now, the most compelling and popular argument against marriage equality is "marriage is between a man and a woman, because the Bible says so."

Not okay.

You can be opposed to marriage equality, but under the political system I'm suggesting politicians would have to debate it with secular reasoning that can appeal to people of all belief systems (like the members of their constituencies they are supposed to be representing). A common, secular argument against marriage equality is the "same-sex parents are unhealthy for kids" one. Fair enough. Let's debate that. That's something we can all agree is important, and something that can be approached with research and logic (and has been) to find a solution that's best for the country as a whole.

Removing the religious crutch in political debates and discussions will do a number of helpful things:

1. It will create a common denominator. Many issues are so religiously loaded that it's near-impossible for people of varying faiths to discuss them without the "discussion" turning into a "whose belief system is better" pissing contest. Let's yell at each other about the issues at hand instead.

2. It will cause people on all sides to think about the issues critically. Whether you know what is right because of your religion, or you know it's wrong because a particular religion shouldn't matter, knowing is the problem. In order to have an actual debate to figure out what's right,

people need to know a bit less and be willing to wonder and examine a bit more.

3. It will turn down the heat. I was always taught that it's impolite to discuss religion or politics at a dinner party. Why is it that we think it's helpful to merge the two into one supercharged, emotionally-unstable, multi-headed media monstrosity? If we can separate the two concepts, at least in discourse, it'll help—at least we'll only be pushing one hot-button at a time.

Removing the religious crutch in political debates and discussions will also not do a number of things (consider this my pre-defense to the comments/emails I know I'm going to get):

1. It will NOT create an immoral, Ayn Randian, dystopic society. In fact, I would argue it will help prevent us from this. Removing religion from political discourse doesn't remove morality or value-based decision-making.

2. It will NOT lead to persecution of Christians. Unless you're one of those who already think this is happening.

3. It will NOT slippery slope now we're marrying toasters and we elected a game of Hungry Hungry Hippos to office and other similar nonsense. Seriously, the "slippery slope Hungry Hungry Hippos" argument is so lazy.

So that's it. Mull it over. Discuss it with a friend. Bring it up to your religious congregation. Then, once we're all onboard, let's do it!

Also, if you're going to email me (my inbox is always open), please refrain from telling me I'm going to burn in hell. It's not that it ruins my day reading dozens of those emails (it does), it's just that I don't know how to respond to them ("thanks for the heads up"?).

> *"The Illinois bureaucracy is on a six-year (so far) unholy war to force two pharmacists who own their own businesses to stock and dispense the 'Plan B' or 'morning-after' drug or close their businesses."*

Pharmacists Should Have the Right to Refuse to Dispense Certain Medications

David Addington

In the following viewpoint, David Addington argues that by requiring pharmacists to stock and provide emergency contraceptives to their customers, the state of Illinois has infringed on the religious liberty of pharmacists who have religious objections to the drugs. At the time of this writing, David Addington was group vice president for research at the Heritage Foundation.

"Why Does the Illinois Government Oppose the Religious Liberty of Pharmacists?" by David Addington, The Heritage Foundation, April 7, 2011. Reprinted by permission.

As you read, consider the following questions:

1. What, according to this viewpoint, is the Illinois government's reasoning for requiring pharmacists to provide any drug that is prescribed for a patient, even if they don't approve?
2. What is the Illinois Health Care Right of Conscience Act described here?
3. Does the situation described in this viewpoint seem to pit two fundamental rights against one another? If so, which two?

The government of Illinois does not understand the importance of, and the legal protections for, religious liberty. The law protects the right of conscience of health care providers, but the Illinois bureaucracy is on a six-year (so far) unholy war to force two pharmacists who own their own businesses to stock and dispense the "Plan B" or "morning-after" drug or close their businesses. Their consciences, based on their religious beliefs, do not allow them to stock and dispense the drug.

The bureaucracy of the state of Illinois established a rule (which it has issued in four versions from 2005 to 2010) that a pharmacy must dispense the drug known as "Plan B" or the "morning-after pill," and called an "emergency contraceptive" under the Illinois rule, upon receipt of a valid prescription. Then-Governor Rod Blagojevich stated in a 2005 press release:

- If a pharmacy wants to be in the business of dispensing contraceptives, then it must fill prescriptions without making moral judgments. Pharmacists—like everyone else—are free to hold personal religious beliefs, but pharmacies are not free to let those beliefs stand in the way of their obligation to their customers.[1]

State officials publicly declared that they would vigorously prosecute pharmacists with religious objections to drive them out of the profession and that a pharmacy must fill Plan B prescriptions without making moral judgments if it wants to stay in business.[2]

Pharmacist Luke Vander Bleek describes himself as a lifelong Catholic with a baccalaureate degree in pharmacy who "has formed a professional opinion 'about teratogenic or abortifacient drugs and their destruction of what he considers is human life,'" believes that "Plan B has an 'abortifacient mechanism of action,'" and believes that "life begins at conception."[3] Pharmacist Glen Kosirog describes himself as a lifelong Christian with a baccalaureate degree in pharmacy who "has formed a professional opinion 'about teratogenic or abortifacient drugs and their destruction of what he considers is human life'" and believes that "Plan B has an 'abortifacient mechanism of action, i.e., [it] can cause abortions by preventing an already fertilized egg from implanting in the womb.'"[4]

The two pharmacists asked an Illinois court to issue an order preventing the state officials from enforcing the rule against them and their respective pharmacies, but the state officials argued that the pharmacists had not followed administrative procedures for complaints and therefore could not be heard in court. The state officials fought the pharmacists all the way through the Illinois court system to the Supreme Court of Illinois, which, by a 5–2 vote, held, on December 18, 2008, that the pharmacists were entitled to their day in court.[5] The State Supreme Court sent the case back down to the trial court to consider the religious conscience claims in the case. The trial court has now issued its decision.

The Circuit Court of the Seventh Judicial Circuit (Sangamon County) of Illinois conducted a trial and, on April 5, 2011, ruled in favor of the pharmacists. The Circuit Court set forth its findings of facts and conclusions of law in an opinion that vindicated religious liberty.

The Circuit Court found that Messrs. Vander Bleek and Kosirog (referred to as the "Plaintiffs") have "sincere religious and conscience-based objections to participating in any way in the distribution of emergency contraceptives."[6] The Court further found that the state rule "imposes financial harms by making it more difficult for Plaintiffs to recruit employees (causing one Plaintiff pharmacy to close) and plan their businesses."[7]

Although the current version of the Illinois rule requires dispensation of all drugs approved by the federal Food and Drug Administration, and not merely emergency contraceptives as did the first three versions, the Circuit Court found that "the focus on emergency contraceptives is still apparent" and that the idea for a broader rule occurred "not because of any problems experienced with other drugs . . . but because" a senior state official "saw a similar rule in an emergency contraceptives case" in another court.[8] The Circuit Court noted that the trial revealed "no evidence of a single person who ever was unable to obtain emergency contraception because of a religious objection" and that

PHARMACISTS MUST PUT PATIENT CARE BEFORE RELIGIOUS BELIEFS

Secularists have urged the General Pharmaceutical Council to ensure that pharmacists set aside their personal religious beliefs if they conflict with a patient's medical needs.

Writing in a consultation response to the General Pharmaceutical Council (GPhC) on "Standards for pharmacy professionals," the Secular Medical Forum said granting unrestricted rights to pharmacy professionals to express their own views places the rights of people who use pharmacy services at risk.

Secular medics said the professional standards must do more than call for "balance" between a pharmacist's "personal values and beliefs" and the "care they give people who use pharmacy services."

The SMF said that this language was "unhelpful" and "ambiguous" because of how "balance" could be interpreted by pharmacists.

"There is a significant risk that those pharmacy professionals with strong personal views, almost always religious" will favour their "own personal views," the Forum warned.

"The result of this may be care determined by the beliefs and values of the professional rather than person-centred care. This risks disadvantaging the person trying to access pharmacy services the state government did not "provide any evidence that anyone was having difficulties finding willing sellers of over-the-counter Plan B, either at pharmacies or over the internet."[9] The Circuit Court also found that the Vander Bleek and Kosirog pharmacies "are within either reasonably close walking or driving distance to emergency contraception distributors, and that emergency contraception is also available over the internet" and further that the state government "conceded that any health impact from Plaintiffs' religious objections would be minimal."[10]

The Circuit Court concluded that the Illinois rule requiring Messrs. Vander Bleek and Kosirog to dispense Plan B violated the Illinois Health Care Right of Conscience Act, the Illinois Religious Freedom Restoration Act, and the federal right to free exercise of

whose own values and beliefs may be overlooked in favour of those of the pharmacy professional."

The Forum called for the GPhC to provide greater clarity in their new guidance by giving examples to pharmacists and "clear advice" for situations "where conflict arises between a pharmacy professional's own views and that of a person accessing services."

If there is a conflict, the SMF said, "person-centred professional care relies on pharmacy professionals setting aside their own personal beliefs where necessary."

The SMF argued that in some circumstances religious objections could not be worked around.

Antony Lempert, chair of the SMF, said: "Where a lone pharmacist is working in a rural community it would be unacceptable to refuse to dispense or to try to redirect a patient to another pharmacy. The responsibility here lies mainly with the pharmacist who has such objections to make sure they do not accept a job which would place them in this predicament."

"There is a fundamental and important distinction between holding a belief and the unrestricted expression of that belief," he said.

"Pharmacists Must Put Patient Care Before Religious Beliefs," National Secular Society, June 29, 2016.

religion guaranteed by the First and Fourteenth Amendments to the US Constitution.

The Illinois Health Care Right of Conscience Act makes it the public policy of Illinois to "respect and protect the right of conscience of all persons . . . who are engaged in . . . the delivery of . . . health care services and medical care" and provides that no health care personnel shall be liable to any person for "refusal to . . . participate in any way in any particular form of health care service which is contrary to the conscience of such . . . health care personnel."[11] The Circuit Court held that the state rule requiring Vander Bleek and Kosirog to dispense Plan B "violates Plaintiffs' rights under the Conscience Act, which was designed to forbid the government from doing what it aims to do here: coercing individuals or entities to provide healthcare services that violate their beliefs."[12]

The Illinois Religious Freedom Restoration Act provides that "Government may not substantially burden a person's exercise of religion, even if the burden results from a rule of general applicability, unless it demonstrates that application of the burden to the person (i) is in furtherance of a compelling governmental interest and (ii) is the least restrictive means of furthering that compelling governmental interest."[13] The Circuit Court held that Vander Bleek and Kosirog "have established the existence of a substantial burden on their religion as to all versions of the Rule," that "[t]he government has not carried its burden of proving that forcing participation by these Plaintiffs is the least restrictive means of furthering a compelling interest," and that the state government had not "demonstrated narrow tailoring, or that there are no less restrictive ways to improve access, such as by providing the drug directly, or using its websites, phone numbers, and signs to help customers find willing sellers." The Circuit Court therefore held that the state rule "violates the Illinois Religious Freedom Restoration Act."[14]

The First Amendment to the US Constitution provides that "Congress shall make no law respecting an establishment of religion, or prohibiting the free exercise thereof," and the US Supreme Court has held the prohibition applicable to the states by virtue of the Fourteenth Amendment prohibition that no state shall "deprive any person of life, liberty, or property, without due process of law."[15] The Circuit Court ruled that, for the same reasons that the state rule violated the compelling interest test under the Illinois Religious Freedom Restoration Act, it also failed the compelling interest test applicable to, and therefore violated, the federal right to free exercise of religion.

Then-Governor Blagojevich and other state officials plainly had little respect for the rights of religious liberty guaranteed by Illinois and federal law. The Circuit Court has made clear that Illinois and federal law protect the rights of conscience of pharmacists Vander Bleek and Kosirog, and the state has admitted that the pharmacists' refusal based on conscience to dispense the Plan B drug does not prevent people from obtaining the Plan B drug and does not have any health impact.

Why, then, do the current governor and other state officials in Illinois continue to press the two pharmacists either to act contrary to their religious beliefs and dispense the drug or to go out of business as the price of following their religious beliefs?

The Governor of Illinois, the Secretary of the Illinois Department of Financial and Professional Regulation, the Acting Director of the Illinois Division of Professional Regulation, and the Illinois State Board of Pharmacy should accept the Circuit Court's injunction against forcing the pharmacists to violate their religious beliefs. They should not appeal the injunction. They should end the state government's multi-year effort to crush the faith-based consciences of Luke Vander Bleek and Glen Kosirog.

Perhaps most importantly in the long run, Illinois Governor Pat Quinn should take appropriate steps to ensure that the executive branch of the Illinois government hereafter shows proper respect for the religious liberty guaranteed to the people by the Constitutions and laws of the United States and Illinois.

Endnotes

1. Press Release by Governor Rod Blagojevich of Illinois, April 13, 2005, cited by the Illinois Supreme Court in *Morr-Fitz, Inc. v. Blagojevich*, 231 Ill. 2d 474, 482 (2008) (hereafter "Illinois Supreme Court Decision").
2. Illinois Supreme Court Decision, p. 501.
3. Illinois Supreme Court Decision, pp. 478–479. The Supreme Court of Illinois noted that the federal Food and Drug Administration acknowledges with respect to the Plan B drug that "[if] fertilization does occur, Plan B may prevent a fertilized egg from attaching to the womb." Ibid., p. 480, n. 1.
4. Illinois Supreme Court Decision, p. 479.
5. Illinois Supreme Court Decision, pp. 504–505 ("[W]e believe that plaintiffs' claims are ripe and that plaintiffs were not required to exhaust administrative remedies.").
6. *Morr-Fitz, Inc. v. Blagojevich*, Case No. 2005-CH-000495 (Circuit Court of the Seventh Judicial Circuit, Sangamon County, Illinois April 5, 2011)(hereafter "Illinois Circuit Court Decision"), slip opinion, p. 2.
7. Illinois Circuit Court Decision, p. 2.
8. Illinois Circuit Court Decision, p. 3.
9. Illinois Circuit Court Decision, pp. 3–4.
10. Illinois Circuit Court Decision, p. 4.
11. 745 Ill. Comp. Stats. 70/2 and 70/4. The statute defines "conscience" to mean "a sincerely held set of moral convictions arising from belief in and relation to God, or which, though not so derived, arises from a place in the life of its possessor parallel to that filled by God among adherents to religious faiths." Ibid. 70/3(e).
12. Illinois Circuit Court Decision, p. 5.
13. 775 Ill. Comp. Stats. 35/15.
14. Illinois Circuit Court Decision, pp. 5–6.
15. *Wallace v. Jaffree*, 472 US 38, 49 (1985). ("As is plain from its text, the First Amendment was adopted to curtail the power of Congress to interfere with the individual's freedom to believe, to worship, and to express himself in accordance with the dictates of his own conscience. Until the Fourteenth Amendment was added to the Constitution, the First Amendment's restraints on the exercise of federal power simply did not apply to the States. But when the Constitution was amended to prohibit any State from depriving any person of liberty without due process of law, that Amendment imposed the same substantive limitations on the States' power to legislate that the First Amendment had always imposed on the Congress' power. This Court has confirmed and endorsed this elementary proposition of law time and time again." [footnotes omitted])

> *"Workers who decline to provide
> treatment run the risk of
> alienating peers."*

Personal Beliefs Can Pit Health Care Workers Against Patients and Colleagues

John Rossheim

In the following viewpoint, John Rossheim goes beyond pharmacists and points out that the refusal, due to personal religious beliefs, of health care workers to provide care for patients doesn't only deny the rights of those patients. It also can cause conflict between the health care workers and their peers and potentially damage the careers of health care workers who refuse to give care. John Rossheim is a journalist covering health care, careers, and workplace issues.

As you read, consider the following questions:

1. How, according to this viewpoint, can refusing to give care alienate health care workers from their colleagues?
2. Based on the sources cited in this viewpoint, what should people with strong religious beliefs about issues such as abortion and homosexuality do when considering a career in health care?
3. What does the author mean when he says "anecdotal evidence" indicates that more health care workers are refusing care on religious grounds?

"Personal Beliefs Can Pit Healthcare Workers Against Patients and Colleagues," by John Rossheim, Monster Worldwide. Reprinted by permission.

An EMT instructed to transport a woman to an abortion clinic declines, citing personal beliefs. A nurse ordered to administer a large dose of morphine to a terminal cancer patient in pain refuses, saying the medication could hasten death. A physician turns away a gay patient, apparently on the basis of his sexual orientation.

Are these scenarios examples of healthcare workers asserting their right of individual conscience, or are they unethical, perhaps illicit denials of patients' rights to receive medically appropriate treatments?

This question is at the center of a simmering debate that is moving beyond pharmacists who refuse to dispense contraceptives to other hot-button issues, such as in vitro fertilization, physician-assisted suicide and stem-cell research, affecting a wide variety of specialties in healthcare. Although there's no reliable statistical evidence that more US healthcare workers are refusing to treat on moral grounds, anecdotal evidence indicates the phenomenon is growing. A variety of bills and laws, mainly on the state level, either grant or deny healthcare workers the right to refuse treatment.

Healthcare Workers' Conscience vs. Patients' Rights

The disagreement is deeply entrenched.

"This is a conflict of the constitutionally based right of conscience and the patient's right of convenience," says Dr. David Stevens, executive director of the Christian Medical & Dental Associations.

Others say healthcare workers who refuse to provide treatment are breaching their professional duty to put the patient first.

Present and future healthcare workers need to know that these legal, ethical and ideological battles threaten to alter professional relationships and change career arcs.

Employer-Employee Communication Makes a Difference

Partisans on both sides say it's important for healthcare workers to inform their employers about what procedures they won't perform—before they are asked to perform them. Some jurisdictions require such notification.

"A California law requires that pharmacists reveal to their employers which treatments they won't provide," says Judy Waxman, vice president for health and reproductive rights at the National Women's Law Center.

Conversely, healthcare employers have a duty to inform job candidates if they won't tolerate treatment refusals. "Companies need to lay out the terms of the job and the expectations when workers are hired," says Arthur Caplan, director of the University of Pennsylvania Center for Bioethics.

Some assert that Title VII of the Civil Rights Act of 1964 forces employers to share the burden of reconciling workers' beliefs with patients' rights. "When an employee makes a request based on religious belief, the employer must attempt a reasonable accommodation but need not take on an undue hardship," says Francis Manion, senior counsel for the American Center for Law & Justice, which represents healthcare workers who have refused to treat.

Still, workers who decline to provide treatment run the risk of alienating peers. "Coworkers will think you're nuts or evil, but that's just how life is," says Kevin McDonnell, a philosophy professor at all-female Saint Mary's College, which is affiliated with the Roman Catholic Church, and a specialist in medical ethics.

Personal Beliefs May Impact Career Choices

Those considering a healthcare career or job change should reflect on how their beliefs align with potential job duties. "Some medical students are required to do abortions, and most of our premed students won't do them, so they're going to have a big fight," McDonnell says.

On the other hand, healthcare workers who believe they must provide any medically appropriate treatment may find themselves curtailed in some settings.

"If you go and work in a Catholic hospital, you are under Catholic healthcare directives, [and] you're ruled by what the bishops and the pope say," Waxman says. "Healthcare workers need to know how their activities may be limited by these directives."

Treatment of Gays and Lesbians Is Also a Battleground

Some healthcare providers deny or limit the care they provide gays and lesbians. "I may not approve of homosexuality, but that doesn't mean I don't treat them," Stevens says. "But I don't help homosexuals conceive children."

Says Jennifer Pizer, senior counsel for Lambda Legal, which advocates for the rights of gays and lesbians: "There's a great obligation on the part of a religious believer to find an occupation where their practice won't injure third parties," such as lesbian patients seeking artificial insemination. "Having a religious motive for the conduct doesn't take away the harm."

Periodical and Internet Sources Bibliography

The following articles have been selected to supplement the diverse views presented in this chapter.

Randall Balmer, "The Johnson Amendment and the First Amendment: A No-Nonsense Protection," *Liberty* magazine, January/February 2018. http://libertymagazine.org/article/the-johnson-amendment-and-the-first-amendment-a-no-nonsense-protection

Rod Dreher, "Christians Can No Longer Be Pharmacists," *American Conservative*, June 28, 2016. https://www.theamericanconservative.com/dreher/christians-can-no-longer-be-pharmacists/

Emma Green, "Even Christian Pharmacists Have to Stock Plan B," *Atlantic*, June 29, 2016. https://www.theatlantic.com/politics/archive/2016/06/pharmacists-have-to-sell-emergency-contracptioneven-if-it-violates-their-religious-beliefs/489182/

Louise P. King and Alan Penzias, "Fostering Discussion When Teaching Abortion and Other Morally and Spiritually Charged Topics," *AMA Journal of Ethics*, July 2018. https://journalofethics.ama-assn.org/article/fostering-discussion-when-teaching-abortion-and-other-morally-and-spiritually-charged-topics/2018-07

Alison Kodjak, "New Trump Rule Protects Health Care Workers Who Refuse Care for Religious Reasons," NPR.org, May 2, 2019. https://www.npr.org/sections/health-shots/2019/05/02/688260025/new-trump-rule-protects-health-care-workers-who-refuse-care-for-religious-reason

Harold G. Koenig, "Religion, Spirituality, and Medicine: How Are They Related and What Does It Mean?" *Mayo Clinic Proceedings*, December 1, 2001. https://www.mayoclinicproceedings.org/article/S0025-6196(11)62793-6/fulltext

Kate Lipman, "Is the Johnson Amendment Constitutional?" Dome blog of the Boston University School of Law, May 20, 2020. http://sites.bu.edu/dome/2020/05/20/is-the-johnson-amendment-constitutional/

Harris Meyer, "Trump's Religious Conscience Rule for Providers Gets Blocked Nationally," *Modern Healthcare*, November 6, 2019. https://www.modernhealthcare.com/law-regulation/trumps -religious-conscience-rule-providers-gets-blocked-nationally

Salvador Rizzo, "President Trump's Shifting Claim that 'We Got Rid of' the Johnson Amendment," *Washington Post*, May 9, 2019. https://www.washingtonpost.com/politics/2019/05/09/president -trumps-shifting-claim-that-we-got-rid-johnson-amendment/

LaShawn Y. Warren, "Three Reasons the Johnson Amendment Should Not Be Repealed," *American Progress*, April 6, 2017. https://www.americanprogress.org/issues/religion /news/2017/04/06/430104/3-reasons-johnson-amendment -not-repealed/

CHAPTER 3

Should Exceptions Be Made for Religious Practices That Are Otherwise Illegal?

Chapter Preface

For all of US history, Americans of all political persuasions have generally agreed that religious liberty should be protected. The freedom to worship as one pleases is deeply embedded in not only the US Constitution but in the history and culture of the nation. When it comes to working out the details of what that freedom means and how it is best protected, however, opinions start to diverge and issues can become quite contentious.

The authors in this chapter confront a question that is far more subtle and complex than it at first seems: If the practices of a religion are in violation of other laws, does freedom of religion require that an exception be made? This issue has come up in the case of religions that use illegal drugs as a part of their ceremonies, and the courts have generally given a great deal of latitude to the religious groups who use these drugs.

In other cases, the question is still being debated and the reasoning is not so clear. In the previous chapter, we examined the questions of whether health care providers should be allowed to refuse to provide health care if they perceive the particular health care service (abortion, certain pain medications) as being contrary to their religious beliefs. Here, the authors take on a similar but more commercial question: Can a business owner discriminate against customers if the store owner disapproves of some aspect of those customers? And what if the entity discriminating is not an individual, but a company—do the same rules apply?

In the following viewpoints, you will read a variety of positions on these issues. The chapter begins with a discussion of the controversies surrounding the Religious Freedom Restoration Act (RFRA), one of those interesting issues that doesn't have clear left-right boundaries.

> *"Opposition to these laws is mounting, thanks to heightened awareness of what RFRAs mean for LGBT rights, religious minorities and the nonreligious, women, and every other group protected under civil rights laws."*

RFRA Creates a Legal Loophole for Discrimination

Freedom from Religion Foundation

In the following viewpoint, the Freedom from Religion Foundation explains what the Religious Freedom Restoration Act (RFRA) is. The author also gives the history of the law and explains why it was passed and why states also passed similar laws. The viewpoint goes on to argue that not only are RFRA laws unnecessary, but they also offer a legal loophole for those who wish to discriminate against others based on religious beliefs. The Freedom from Religion Foundation is an organization dedicated to protecting separation of church and state.

"Religious Freedom Restoration Act (RFRA)," Freedom from Religion Foundation. Reprinted by permission.

As you read, consider the following questions:

1. Why does RFRA act as a "de facto constitutional amendment"?
2. In what way, according to the viewpoint, does the First Amendment already do what RFRA is meant to do?
3. The author argues that the federal RFRA law violates more than just the establishment clause. What other parts of the Constitution does the author say it violates?

The Religious Freedom Restoration Act is a law that allows religious people, businesses, and/or corporations to violate generally applicable laws by claiming that the laws conflict with their religious beliefs. The federal version is written: "Government may substantially burden a person's exercise of religion only if it demonstrates that application of the burden to the person— (1) is in furtherance of a compelling governmental interest; and (2) is the least restrictive means of furthering that compelling governmental interest." Many states have RFRAs too, but those three concepts—burden, compelling governmental interest, and least restrictive means—appear in every single RFRA.

What Is the History Behind RFRA?

In 1990, two practitioners of a Native American religion were fired from their job as drug counselors and ruled ineligible for unemployment benefits because they were using peyote. They challenged the denial, claiming that their religion made them ingest peyote, so the state could not punish them for exercising their religion.

In *Employment Division v. Smith*, the Supreme Court upheld the denial of benefits because the law was not "prohibiting the exercise of religion"; the religious burden was "merely the incidental effect of a generally applicable and otherwise valid provision." 494 US 872 (1990). In other words, the Supreme Court declared that a person's private religious beliefs cannot trump the law.

Religious hysteria exploded after the *Smith* decision, so Congress passed RFRA: a super-statute that effectively amends every other federal law. RFRA essentially acts as a de facto constitutional amendment.

In 1997, the Supreme Court ruled the federal RFRA unconstitutional as applied to the states, but allowed it to continue to apply to federal law. *City of Boerne v. Flores*, 521 US 507 (1997). Since that time, roughly 20 states have enacted their own RFRAs, modeled off the federal law.

What's the Big Deal with RFRAs?

Do you remember the Supreme Court's *Hobby Lobby* decision that allowed for-profit corporations to exercise their so-called "religious conscience" in order to restrict employees' access to contraceptives? Have you been watching the legal battles over cake decorators, florists, and municipal clerks who want to be able to discriminate against gay couples in the name of "religious freedom"?

The federal RFRA law is directly responsible for the Supreme Court's *Hobby Lobby* debacle. State RFRAs, based on the federal version, are emboldening corporations and business owners to discriminate against gay people, religious minorities and the nonreligious, and any other group their religion declares inferior.

Essentially, RFRAs create a legal loophole for anyone who wishes to discriminate in the name of religion, allowing individuals and corporations to be free from following the laws everyone else must follow if they claim it would "burden" their religion. And the bar for what constitutes a burden on religion has been set very low. Here's the causal chain that the Court accepted as a substantial burden on Hobby Lobby's religion:

1. A believes that Drug X violates A's religion
2. A owns a distinct legal entity, Company H
3. Company H buys a health insurance plan for its employees, as required by law
4. H employs Person B

5. Dr. C, B's doctor, recommends and prescribes X for B

6. B personally chooses to take X

7. The company insurance plan pays for X

8. Therefore, A's religion is violated

Additional legal challenges in the wake of *Hobby Lobby* make it clear that there's no burden too small to trigger a religious objection. One organization has claimed that filling out a single-page form with their name, contact information, date, and signature is a burden on their religion. And the purpose of the form, EBSA 700, is simply to notify the IRS that the organization has a religious objection to contraception. How burdensome!

FFRF has been warning against the dangers of RFRAs since before the *Hobby Lobby* case was decided. The good news is that other civil rights groups and pro-equality businesses are waking up and realizing the dangers of these laws. To them we say, welcome to the fight.

What Does RFRA Protect That the First Amendment Doesn't?

The short answer is "nothing." Indiana's recently passed RFRA law makes it all too clear that these laws are not meant to create a shield to protect the religious from persecution. The First Amendment already does this. RFRAs are designed as a sword to allow religious people and corporations to impose their personal religious beliefs onto others. RFRAs are supported by anti-LGBT lobbyists and others who wish to legalize religiously-motivated bigotry.

Aren't Some RFRAs Better Than Others? Indiana's RFRA Is Bad, but Aren't the Others Ok?

Some apologists for the federal RFRA have focused on how RFRAs in states like Indiana differ from the federal law and RFRAs in other states. The truth is that courts have yet to decide whether the minor variations in language state-to-state make any practical legal difference. But more important, debating these nuances misses the larger point: every RFRA creates the same problem by elevating religious belief above the law.

Critics of the original Indiana law pointed out that its language explicitly applied to corporations, appearing to allow businesses to discriminate against minorities. The Indiana Legislature hurriedly added clarifying language stating that businesses cannot discriminate against minorities under the new law, but that amendment merely fixes one of the numerous problems that RFRA creates. The Supreme Court has already decided that businesses can discriminate against women seeking contraceptive coverage under the federal RFRA. Expect more problematic RFRA rulings to come.

Is RFRA Constitutional?

While the Supreme Court's *Hobby Lobby* ruling relied solely on the federal RFRA, rather than on an interpretation of the Constitution, the Court intentionally avoided addressing whether RFRA is itself a constitutional law. FFRF's amicus brief in the case received national attention for being the only brief to argue that RFRA is unconstitutional. Here are the arguments:

1. **RFRA violates the separation of powers.** Our Constitution is based on the principle that government power is divided between three branches, the Executive, Legislative, and Judicial. RFRA is a law passed by Congress that dictates how the judicial branch is supposed to interpret a citizen's right to religious freedom. When the Supreme Court decided *Employment Division v. Smith*, it was exercising judicial power to interpret the First Amendment. Congress didn't like that interpretation, so it passed a law that imposed a new interpretation of religious freedom on every federal statute. RFRA was a slap in the face to the Court.

2. **RFRA violates Article V.** RFRA operates like a constitutional amendment, but was passed like any normal piece of legislation. It's a super-statute that trumps every US law

and regulation, just like the Constitution. It imposes a new interpretative framework that fundamentally changes the law of the land, but wasn't subject to the rigorous procedures our Constitution has in place for constitutional amendments.

3. **RFRA violates the Establishment Clause.** RFRA elevates religious beliefs above the rights of citizens, granting special privileges to those who profess religious beliefs. RFRA favors religious citizens (or corporations run by religious citizens) by granting them exemptions to the law, while disfavoring nonreligious citizens who are required to follow the law.

What Can I Do to Stop RFRA?

You can voice your opposition to the federal RFRA by contacting your members of Congress asking them to repeal RFRA.

JOIN FFRF, which has taken a leadership role in calling for repeal of RFRA, and which will keep you informed of RFRA action in your state. Not only will you stay informed, you will be helping support an organization that has taken action against RFRAs every step of the way.

FFRF has called on governors in every state with an RFRA to work toward repealing those laws. We have also worked with noted state-church attorney and constitutional scholar Marci A. Hamilton to combat the federal RFRA. Opposition to these laws is mounting, thanks to heightened awareness of what RFRAs mean for LGBT rights, religious minorities and the nonreligious, women, and every other group protected under civil rights laws. In addition to supporting FFRF, you can spread the word to ensure that everyone is aware of the threat posed by RFRA.

> *"We need to look behind the religious*
> *fundamentalist intolerance of a*
> *powerful few to recognize that*
> *what's afoot with these RFRAs*
> *is the dramatic expansion of the*
> *civil liberties of corporations in*
> *a coordinated corporate civil*
> *rights movement."*

The Primary Purpose of RFRA Laws Is Not Discrimination, but Corporate Civil Rights

Joseph R. Slaughter

The previous viewpoint argued that RFRA acts provided a back door for legal discrimination. In the following viewpoint, Joseph R. Slaughter does not disagree with that but argues that there is a possibly more dangerous aspect to RFRA laws. The author contends that these laws are an attempt to use religious intolerance to strengthen the civil rights of corporations at the expense of individuals. Joseph R. Slaughter is a professor at Columbia University specializing in literature, law, and sociocultural history.

"Religious Freedom Restoration Acts: What if Inclusion Really Is What They're All About?" by Joseph R. Slaughter, The Social Justice Foundation, April 8, 2015. Reprinted by permission.

As you read, consider the following questions:

1. What does the author mean by "our degraded democracy"?
2. What parts of the law, according to the viewpoint, aren't receiving much notice, and what are the implications for democracy?
3. How have corporations replaced individuals as the beneficiaries of the First Amendment, according to the author?

I happen to be sitting at a desk from the Indiana General Assembly, mulling over the Indiana Religious Freedom Restoration Act. The desk is not in the state legislature; it's an inherited desk, from another political era, given to my grandfather by the State of Indiana in recognition of 18 years of service in the House of Representatives when the chamber was remodeled in 1985. My grandfather began his political career during the civil rights era; he retired during the Reagan years.

As I read the Indiana RFRA, coverage of the protests against it, the amendment to "fix" it, and analysis of the social implications of the law, I can't help but think of my grandfather and of how little he would recognize today's debate and our degraded democracy.

He would have been appalled at the naked attempt to legalize discrimination against any portion of the population—LGBT or otherwise. But I believe he might have been even more outraged at the subtext of the law, the cynical manipulation of religious intolerance, and its veiled attempt to secure the civil rights of corporations. Indeed, when he retired (and later died) in the 1980s, he couldn't have imagined the hostile corporate takeover of civil rights that has been underway in this country over the past three decades.

What if "inclusion" is as dangerous as discrimination?

Let's be clear about these new RFRAs in Indiana, Arkansas, and elsewhere: they do indeed make it legal for private, for-profit businesses to discriminate against lesbians, gays, and others on "religious" grounds. But that may not be the primary purpose of such acts. Such laws feed on some people's prejudices against a minority group to curry popular favor with another minority group; they use the fervor of fear and hatred to pass legislation that under more reasonable circumstances would find little support.

The Indiana RFRA is not simply "the product of a G.O.P. search for a respectable way to oppose same-sex marriage and to rally the base around it," as Amy Davidson put it in the *New Yorker*. We need to look behind the religious fundamentalist intolerance of a powerful few to recognize that what's afoot with these RFRAs is the dramatic expansion of the civil liberties of corporations in a coordinated corporate civil rights movement.

Perhaps this is why Indiana Governor Mike Pence was willing to walk back the discriminatory aspect of the bill in response to the public outcry. It's not because he suddenly saw the light on gay rights. It's because the parts of the law that aren't being protested or receiving any notice accomplish something else that has far-reaching implications for our democracy.

Brian Bosma, speaker of the Indiana House (from where my desk was pulled), introduced a proposed amendment that would "fix" the law, explaining that "what was intended as a message of inclusion of all religious beliefs was interpreted as a message of exclusion, especially for the LGBT community."

Bosma's amendment (signed by Pence on Thursday) may address concerns about discrimination, but it leaves intact the provisions that expand and reinforce the precedent established by the United States Supreme Court decision in the *Hobby Lobby* case. In that case, the activist conservative judges on the Roberts Court pierced the corporate veil in order to grant religious freedoms to for-profit companies.

One reason for creating a corporation is to establish a legal entity that is distinct from its owners and operators in order to separate the financial and moral responsibility of the corporation from the financial and moral responsibilities of its individual

RFRA EXPLAINED

The Religious Freedom Restoration Act (RFRA) is a federal law passed in 1993 that is intended to prevent other federal laws from substantially burdening a person's free exercise of religion. The legislation was introduced by Rep. Chuck Schumer (D-NY) on March 11, 1993 and passed by a unanimous US House and a near unanimous US Senate with three dissenting votes. The bill was signed into law by President Bill Clinton.

The RFRA states that the government shall not substantially burden a person's exercise of religion even if the burden results from a rule of general applicability, unless it is in furtherance of a compelling governmental interest and is the least restrictive means of furthering that compelling governmental interest. A person whose religious exercise has been burdened in violation of this law may assert that violation as a claim or defense in a judicial proceeding and obtain appropriate relief against a government.

executives and shareholders. This is referred to as the "corporate veil," and it ensures that the corporation and the individuals who operate or own it are distinct legal entities—different "persons."

The Court determined that because Hobby Lobby was "closely held" by one family, the company shared its owners' right to religion; the company is Christian, it concluded. Hobby Lobby doesn't attend church, of course; nonetheless, it now practices an official state-sanctioned religion, and it has the right to deny contraceptive coverage to its employees as part of its religious liberty.

The new RFRAs pierce the corporate veil further: Any corporation may be said to have a religion. The Indiana RFRA expands the scope of religious protection to any "for profit or nonprofit" company in which the "individuals" who have "control and substantial ownership of the entity" share "a system of religious belief."

The Indiana law, like the *Hobby Lobby* decision, confuses the corporation with the individual human beings who run it. The language that makes this corporate usurpation of our civil rights

When it was passed in 1993, Congress intended RFRA to apply to all branches of government, and both to federal and state law. But in 1997 in the case of *City of Boerne v. Flores*, the Supreme Court ruled the RFRA exceeded federal power when applied to state laws. In response to this ruling, some individual states passed state-level Religious Freedom Restoration Acts that apply to state governments and local municipalities. Currently, there are 21 states that have passed a Religious Freedom Restoration Act that is based on or is similar to the federal act. Those states are Alabama, Arizona, Arkansas, Connecticut, Florida, Idaho, Illinois, Indiana, Kansas, Kentucky, Louisiana, Mississippi, Missouri, New Mexico, Oklahoma, Pennsylvania, Rhode Island, South Carolina, Tennessee, Texas, and Virginia. Ten other states have religious liberty protections that state courts have interpreted to provide a similar (strict scrutiny) level of protection. Those states are Alaska, Hawaii, Maine, Massachusetts, Michigan, Minnesota, Montana, Ohio, Washington, and Wisconsin.

"5 Facts About the Religious Freedom Restoration Act," by Joe Carter, Ethics and Religious Liberty Commission, January 18, 2018.

possible is in Section 7 of the law: "As used in this chapter, 'person' includes the following: (1) An individual. (2) An organization, a religious society, a church, a body of communicants, or a group organized and operated primarily for religious purposes. (3) A partnership, a limited liability company, a corporation, a company, a firm, a society, a joint-stock company, an unincorporated association...." In this formulation, corporations take advantage of the legal category of "person" to acquire the civil and political rights of human beings—to acquire human rights.

If *Hobby Lobby* put a foot in the door, the new RFRAs are part of the steady march of the corporate civil rights movement, whose allies include the conservative judges on the US Supreme Court. As a recent study by Harvard legal scholar John C. Coates IV reveals, corporations "have begun to displace individuals as the direct beneficiaries of the First Amendment," more effectively claiming rights to religion and speech than have individuals over the past 20 years.

The new RFRAs are part of a pattern that includes the *Citizens United* decision, in which the Supreme Court granted corporations unlimited political free speech rights in the form of monetary contributions to political groups. In doing so, the Court effectively diminished the political power of individuals by increasing the electoral influence of corporations. Indeed, the Court extended to corporations some of the civil rights protections that it weakened for racial minorities by crippling the 1965 Voting Rights Act with its decision in *Shelby County v. Holder.*

To be sure, the Indiana law might not at first look like a corporate takeover of civil rights, in part because it is being successfully protested and in part because many major corporations have joined the critics. Apple and Walmart, for example, quickly lined up on the side of those protesting possible discrimination against same-sex couples that the RFRA legalized. But the fix is in.

Discrimination of any sort is bad business for large corporations. But joining the chorus of anger over the potential discrimination against LGBT persons has hidden benefits for corporations, turning our attention away from the part of the law that is good for businesses but bad for democracy. Indeed, the corporate messages of support for the proposed amendment should alert us to the fact that the underlying law is seen by companies to be advantageous for securing greater civil rights and political power.

It may be a good victory for the civil rights of the LGBT community (and others) that the law is finally amended. But corporations in the US have been taking advantage of the civil rights movements of real people since the abolition era to seize their own civil and political rights. Indeed, a quick victory for equal rights may obscure the longer-term damage being done to our political and legal system by expanding the civil and political rights of corporations, who stand to benefit at our expense even from a "fixed" Restoration of Religious Freedom Act.

My grandfather, Richard D. Bell, was (among other things) a union organizer from La Porte. A Democrat from industrial northwest Indiana, he was alert to corporate power grabs. He would have found Indiana's RFRA despicable, its discriminatory effects intolerable, and its quiet expansion of corporate civil and political rights dangerous to democracy. If only politics and the law were as simple as the desk at which I sit.

> *"Religious belief is sacrosanct under the Constitution. But religiously motivated conduct is not—when it violates civil law."*

RFRA Wrongly Transforms Courts into Legislatures

Marci A. Hamilton

This viewpoint takes a slightly different tack on the issue of RFRA laws and uses a different example to frame the discussion. In the following viewpoint, Marci A. Hamilton also opposes RFRA laws, but her argument is based on a slightly different objection. According to the author, the primary flaw in RFRA laws is that they take the role of legislating out of the hands of legislative bodies and give that role to the courts. Marci A. Hamilton is a professor at the Benjamin N. Cardozo School of Law at Yeshiva University.

As you read, consider the following questions:

1. How is the application of RFRA laws discussed in this viewpoint different from others mentioned earlier?
2. What is the Constitution's Free Exercise Clause, and how is it described here?
3. How does the author distinguish between conduct and belief, and how does this affect her argument?

"A Federal Appeals Court Says a Religious Group Can Import Illegal Drugs: The Religious Freedom Restoration Act Shows Its True Colors," by Marci A. Hamilton, Thomson Reuters, November 18, 2004. Reprinted by permission.

The US Court of Appeals for the Tenth Circuit recently sat en banc—that is, in a larger-than-usual panel representing the Circuit as a whole—to address the claim that the federal drug laws do not apply to a particular church.

The party adverse to the government was the O Centro Espirita Beneficiente Uniao Do Vegetal (UDV). It was secretly importing a tea-like substance called hoasca—which it refers to as the "vine of the soul," the "vine of the dead," and the "vision vine"—from Brazil to the US for use in its religious ceremonies. The problem is, hoasca contains a Controlled Substances Act, Schedule I, banned drug.

Unbelievably, the Tenth Circuit ruled in favor of the UDV. Its ruling (on the likelihood of success on the merits in the context of a preliminary injunction request) purports to foreclose the government from enforcing the drug laws. That's a perversion of the Constitution's Free Exercise Clause, and it cannot be squared with the Supreme Court's free exercise jurisprudence. But it did not have to square with the Free Exercise Clause, because it was brought under the Religious Freedom Restoration Act (RFRA). Interestingly, the panel included Judge Michael McConnell— formerly a law professor highly critical of current Free Exercise doctrine and highly supportive of RFRA.

Generally, of course, we all must abide by the federal drug laws and international treaties prohibiting the importation of illegal use and international trafficking in drugs into the country. So the court's ruling may seem odd: Courts are not normally in the business of deciding whether to enforce a law or not. To the contrary, under the Constitution, they are obligated to enforce the law.

But this case was decided under RFRA. And that misguided statute, as I will explain, wrongly transforms courts into legislatures. Here, for example, the Tenth Circuit—absurdly—used RFRA as the basis to enjoin the federal government's enforcement of the drug laws.

Background on the UDV, Hoasca, and the Case Before the Court

If the reader hasn't heard of the UDV, that may be because, in the United States, it remains a very tiny religious institution.

The UDV was founded in 1963 by a Brazilian rubber-tapper who discovered that hoasca could be made from several plants indigenous to the rainforest. Hoasca, as the Tenth Circuit described it, is a "liquid, tea-like mixture."

The plants from which hoasca is made are *psychotria viridis* and *banisteriposis caapi*. As the Tenth Circuit also explained, *psychotria viridis* "contains dimethyltryptamine (DMT), which is listed on Schedule I of the CSA and the Convention."

The religion is a blend of Christian theology and indigenous American beliefs. In Brazil, it has approximately 8,000 members.

In 1993, one of its leaders arrived here in the United States. And as of now, there are 130 members in the United States. The UDV's ceremonies involving hoasca occur at least twice a month, and last roughly four hours. Church officials prepare the hoasca in Brazil and ship it here for the UDV's ceremonies.

The case before the Tenth Circuit arose because United States Customs Service officials seized approximately 30 gallons of hoasca in transit, and has threatened prosecution. In light of the threat—according to the Tenth Circuit's original panel opinion, issued in September 2003—UDV has ceased using hoasca in the United States.

After the seizure, the UDV filed suit—asking for injunctive relief and a declaratory judgment that its practices are protected under the US Constitution and the Religious Freedom Restoration Act (RFRA). But, as I will explain, it is RFRA—not the Constitution's Free Exercise Clause—that really made the difference in this case. Indeed, RFRA opened the door for the Tenth Circuit en banc panel to become a super-legislature, supposedly competent to determine federal and international drug policy.

Technically, because the subject was a preliminary injunction, what the Tenth Circuit held was that the UDV was substantially likely to succeed in its claims. But the court's analysis made clear that if presented with the issue directly, it would rule for the UDV—and thereby undo neutral federal criminal laws.

The Free Exercise Clause—and How RFRA Tries to Modify It

The Constitution's Free Exercise Clause has long been interpreted to allow neutral laws that regulate conduct—not belief—to be applied to religious persons and institutions, along with everyone else in society. The untenable alternative would be to apply the law regulating conduct to everyone except those who are religiously motivated. But conduct is conduct, and harm is harm.

Religious belief is sacrosanct under the Constitution. But religiously motivated conduct is not—when it violates civil law.

Thus, in the Supreme Court's opinion in *Employment Div. v. Smith*, Native American Church members, who used peyote, a hallucinogen, in their religious ceremonies, were held subject to the state and federal drug laws. Like everyone else, the Court concluded, they were prohibited by law from using hallucinogen—even in religious ceremonies.

The Court noted in its ruling that their remedy was to ask the legislatures—not the court—to modify the law. And indeed, they had already succeeded in some states, as the *Smith* decision explicitly noted. They went on to secure legislative exemptions for the sacramental use of peyote in many states and from Congress. One would have thought that that would have been the end of the story, because the Court's jurisprudence did indeed ensure religious liberty.

After *Smith*, though, a torrent of unwarranted criticism rained down on the Supreme Court—while accommodations for peyote were being secured. The argument was that legislatures could not be trusted to grant exemptions for religious practices. In a move that cannot be explained by logic, but only by politics, Congress, through unanimous consent in the House and a near-unanimous recorded vote in the Senate, passed the Religious Freedom

Restoration Act (RFRA). In effect, RFRA gives religious entities the power to challenge the application of every law in the land—and in so doing, it runs directly contrary to the Supreme Court's Free Exercise doctrine, as embodied in *Smith* and other precedents.

In *Boerne v. Flores*, the Supreme Court struck down RFRA as applied to the states. But so far, the courts have upheld RFRA's application to federal law. They reason that a government can place whatever restraints it imposes on itself.

But they ignore how RFRA places courts into the constitutional shoes of the legislatures. RFRA appoints courts to become the primary drafters of public policy, when that is the province of legislatures. And it infringes on the Supreme Court's—and lower federal courts'—power to interpret the Constitution by displacing the Court's own interpretation of Free Exercise Clause, and replacing it with Congress's preferred interpretation.

RFRA's Three-Part Analysis, as Applied in the UDV/Hoasca Case

Specifically, a court applying RFRA must go through a three-part analysis:

First, it must ask whether the religious institution or person has shown that the law imposes a substantial burden, which is to say that it must make the practice "effectively impracticable." That was obviously the case with the UDV and hoasca: If the church couldn't legally import the drug, it couldn't use it in its ritual.

Second, it must ask if the government has proven its law satisfies a compelling interest. Plainly, the interest in keeping illegal drugs out of the US is compelling.

Third, and crucially, the court must ask whether the laws enforced are the least restrictive means the government can opt for, with respect to this particular believer. This third step was crucial in the UDV/hoasca case.

The Key to the Tenth Circuit's Ruling: The "Least Restrictive Means" Step

Here, the laws at issue were the Controlled Substances Act, and the United Nations Convention on Psychotropic Substances. (The Convention, which provides for the cooperation of nations in their attempts to eliminate the illicit use and trafficking in psychotropic substances, also is part of US law, for the Constitution deems treaties to be part of US law.)

The Tenth Circuit had to ask whether these laws were the least restrictive means the federal government could have chosen, with respect to the UDV believers.

Judge Murphy, in dissent, wisely said yes. But Judges Seymour and McConnell said no (in separate opinions, neither of which garnered the support of a majority of the court).

Judges Seymour and McConnell's Fallacy: Using Evidence for Legislative Exemption

In so holding, Judges Seymour and McConnell assessed the evidence from a hearing before the district court and concluded that by their lights there should be an exemption for the UDV.

Judge Seymour even suggested, shockingly, that a treaty exemption could be judge-made! She pointed out that the relevant Convention permitted signatory nations to obtain an exemption from the treaty for prohibited substances "traditionally used by certain small, clearly determined groups in magical or religious rites." She then pointed out that the United States obtained just such an exemption for the Native American Church for peyote. But she omitted a glaring truth: The United States had not done so for the UDV—as of yet. And hoasca is not peyote.

Her opinion, though, did reveal that UDV had two other options open to it. Free exercise doctrine permits exemptions in the legislatures and the Convention permits an exemption as well. So what RFRA has done is to detour religious entities from the political process where they would have to justify their need for exemption in the light of the public good into a courtroom where it is impossible for the government to gin up the sort of legislative record—hearings, reports from experts, investigations—that could only justify a conclusion regarding whether to permit use of a Schedule I drug.

Judge McConnell's opinion (joined by Judge Tymkovich) is the quintessential example of the court as super-legislature. He rejected explicit Congressional findings regarding Schedule I drugs, like hoasca, because they cannot be "conclusive." He asserted, for instance, that "Congress's inclusion of DMT in Schedule I "should [not] control our assessment of the relative dangerousness of hoasca," because Congress had not considered hoasca by itself. But why not? Congress doubtless included DMT because it found it dangerous. And hoasca contains DMT.

McConnell also complained that "Congressional findings invariably tout the importance of the laws to which they are appended." And he criticized the particular findings Congress chose to make in this case: "If Congress or the executive branch had investigated the religious use of hoasca and had come to an informed conclusion that the health risks or possibility of diversion were sufficient to outweigh free exercise concerns in this case, that conclusion would be entitled to great weight."

It did not matter to McConnell that the findings Congress made were good enough for Congress, which is, after all, charged with making the law, and which was, deciding whether to pass a neutral drug law, not whether to grant an exemption. Nor did it matter under McConnell's RFRA analysis that the UDV could easily seek that very exemption from Congress—and submit evidence in support of that exemption at that time.

Congress, Not the Courts, Should Be the Ones to Decide on Drug Law Exemptions

There are important separation of powers reasons for why courts should not be carving out exemptions that are within the sole power of other bodies—including Congress. As Judge Murphy remarked, assessing the evidence to decide whether a given exemption should be granted is the function of the legislature—not the court.

Judge McConnell response to Judge Murphy's argument was this: If the court were institutionally incompetent in the drug laws, "the same may be said for application of RFRA to virtually any field of regulation that may conflict with religious exercise."

McConnell seemed to see this consequence as an absurdity. But it is simply the truth.

RFRA is unconstitutional, under the separation of powers, precisely because an institutionally incompetent branch, the judiciary, has been assigned the duty of a competent branch, Congress—in this case, the core duty to make the law.

Yet courts are in no position to make the public policy determination whether a drug can or should be permitted for some groups and not others. They are inherently institutionally incompetent to do so, as they must make decisions within the narrow confines of a particular case under only the facts presented by two parties.

No court in the country is capable of seeing the big picture that is essential in making decisions on public policy—including decisions on whether to grant exemptions from a generally applicable law, and whether they will erode the general law's effectiveness or result in harm to others. Only the legislature—with its wide-ranging fact-finding capacities and its charge to make the laws in the public good—can be trusted to do this.

Republicans, Especially, Should Oppose This Kind of Judicial Overreaching

During the last election, Republicans frequently talked about the need for judges to interpret the law, not make it. Hear, hear.

But RFRA invites judges to do just the opposite; it encourages judicial activists like McConnell to appoint themselves superlegislatures, and to second-guess what the people's representatives have done or should do. For this reason, among others, the Republican-controlled Congress should repeal RFRA—

or it will continue to deputize the very kind of activism by judges that Republicans hate. It's not surprising that RFRA aligns itself with a more liberal agenda; its standard of strict scrutiny in free exercise cases involving neutral, generally applicable laws was devised by Justice William Brennan.

And the need for RFRA simply cannot be proven. There are hundreds, if not thousands of legislative religious exemptions in the United States. They grant everything from an exemption to the felony murder laws for faith-healing parents who permit their children to die, to an exemption from the immunization laws for school-age children for parents who oppose immunization on religious grounds.

Whatever the wisdom of these particular exemptions, they testify to the ability of religious organizations—even small ones—to work within the system, and to obtain exemptions from legislatures. The UDV should not have been able to invoke the courts to obtain the right to avoid the drug laws. RFRA as applied to federal law plainly violates the separation of powers, and no case illustrates this fact better than this one.

> "The principle of religious liberty should extend to all people, not only ones who come from a specific set of religious beliefs."

RFRA Was Not Intended as a Tool for Discrimination

Emily London and Maggie Siddiqi

In the following excerpted viewpoint, Emily London and Maggie Siddiqi open with an in-depth discussion of the origin of RFRA laws. The authors go on to argue that rather than protecting religious liberty, the Hobby Lobby *case and RFRA laws actually privilege one type of religion (Protestant Christianity) over others, a clear violation of the Establishment Clause. This was not, they contend, the purpose of these laws, and they advocate for an amendment that would rectify the problem. Emily London is a research assistant for the Faith and Progressive Policy Initiative at the Center for American Progress. Maggie Siddiqi is the director of the Faith and Progressive Policy Initiative at the Center for American Progress.*

"Religious Liberty Should Do No Harm," by Emily London and Maggie Siddiqi, Center for American Progress, April 11, 2019. Reprinted by permission.

As you read, consider the following questions:

1. How does the use of data on the religious demographics in the United States help the authors make their case?
2. What solutions do the authors offer for the harm RFRA laws have caused?
3. How would these changes help people of all faiths, including Protestant Christians, according to the viewpoint?

Twenty-five years ago, the federal Religious Freedom Restoration Act (RFRA) was signed into law to clarify and expand upon the right to religious liberty. RFRA outlines that the government "should not substantially burden religious exercise without compelling justification" and that it should only do so if it furthers a compelling governmental interest in the least restrictive way possible.[1] The purpose of this law is "to protect the free exercise of religion" while clearly defining and more robustly protecting the right of religious liberty for all Americans.[2] It passed with widespread, bipartisan support and was triumphed among faith communities, civil rights advocates, and politicians alike.[3] Since the passing of the federal RFRA, 21 states have mirrored the federal statute to adopt similar legislation.[4]

In 2014, however, the US Supreme Court decision in *Burwell v. Hobby Lobby* marked a major shift in the interpretation of religious exemptions from religiously neutral laws. Rather than simply protecting the rights of religious people, RFRA was expanded and misused to discriminate. By treating two for-profit corporations—craft chain Hobby Lobby and furniture-maker Conestoga Wood Specialties—like individuals with the right to free exercise of religion, the ruling allowed the religious beliefs of the company owners to override those of their employees, rescinding employees' access to no-cost contraceptive health coverage to which they are entitled under federal law.[5] The ruling affected thousands of employees, and it expanded the use of religious exemptions by redefining the scope of federal RFRA protections to include for-profit corporations. The legacy of the *Hobby Lobby* decision has continued under the Trump administration as religious liberty is misused to discriminate against vulnerable communities, such as religious minorities, nonreligious people, people of color, women, and the LGBTQ community.[6]

The United States was founded on the principle of religious liberty—a principle that is now under threat. At the nation's outset, lawmakers established a unique society without a government-established religion, which is cemented in the First Amendment to the Constitution, and sanctioned rights for religious people.[7] They also protected the rights of religious institutions and ensured that all Americans could express a diverse range of beliefs without interference from the government.[8] In recent years, however, the right to religious liberty has increasingly been exploited and misused in order to favor the interests of select, privileged conservative Protestant Christians over the basic rights of the most vulnerable Americans.[9]

The principle of religious liberty should extend to all people, not only ones who come from a specific set of religious beliefs. A 2014 study from the Pew Research Center reveals that the religious landscape in the United States is changing.[10] As the Christian population is declining—particularly among mainline Protestants and Catholics—the number of adults who do not identify with a specific religion is growing.[11] With the changing demographics of Americans and their religious connections, it is even more important that people of all faiths and people of no faith are granted the fundamental right to religious liberty.

Protecting religious liberty continues to be a priority for a majority of Americans: Almost two-thirds believe that there should be a "strict separation" between church and state, and nine out of 10 agree that the United States was founded with universal religious freedom that extends to people of all religions.[12] Policymakers have an opportunity and a responsibility to enact policies that will ensure the right of religious liberty for all Americans without infringing on the rights and religious freedoms of others.

[…]

Data suggest a disconnect between which religious groups believe that their religious liberty is being threatened and those who are actually subject to the most harm due to religious discrimination. Most Americans do not believe that religious liberty is currently being threatened in America.[81] However, a majority of white evangelical Protestants—69 percent—disagree and believe that religious liberty is under threat.[82] In addition, 57 percent of white evangelical Protestants believe that Christians face discrimination in America, while only 44 percent of the same group believe that Muslims face discrimination.[83] Though white evangelical Protestants perceive victimization most strongly, other religious groups are being harmed by religious-based discrimination, and even hate crimes, more frequently. Analysis of FBI hate crime data from 2017 reveals that almost 80 percent of all incidents of religiously motivated hate crimes that year were motivated by anti-Jewish or anti-Muslim bias.[84] Yet both the executive and judicial branches of government have prioritized the alleged discrimination faced by some white evangelical Protestants over the outsized number of threats that other groups face.

[…]

Policies and Practices to Reinstate a Balanced and Inclusive Vision of Religious Liberty

Policymakers at all levels have the opportunity to create structures for a more balanced vision of religious liberty in America. Legislative options at the federal and state levels can explicitly codify nondiscrimination protections, while initiatives at the local level can pave the way for future policies and greater levels of public understanding. Most importantly, policies must respect religious beliefs without harming or infringing on the rights of others. Through options like the examples below, policymakers can create the framework for a balanced, inclusive vision of religious liberty throughout the United States.

Clarify That RFRA Is Not Intended to Be a Tool to Discriminate

The recently reintroduced Do No Harm Act would amend the federal RFRA to prohibit granting exemptions to civil rights laws that could cause third-party harm.[90] It would help to ensure that populations particularly vulnerable to the abuse of religious liberty are legally protected from such discrimination. Moreover, it would help to restore a balanced interpretation of religious liberty in which laws serve as a shield for religious freedom and religion cannot be used as a justification for discrimination.

State RFRAs should explicitly balance religious protections with nondiscrimination language.[91] For example, Texas' RFRA contains provisions to ensure that it is not used to avoid pre-existing civil rights protections, stating: "The protection of religious freedom afforded by this chapter is in addition to the protections provided under federal law and the constitutions of this state and the United States."[92] New state RFRAs should include specific language outlining the limits of the RFRA so that vulnerable communities are not put at risk. Meanwhile, existing state RFRAs should look to add similar language.

Ensure That Religious Exemptions Do Not Undermine Patient Health

All hospitals should be required to clearly provide a list of services that they do not offer. For example, Washington state requires that hospitals make this information accessible on their websites—only posting it on the corporate parent site is not acceptable. As is the case in Washington, this information should be "readily accessible to the public, without requiring a login or other restriction."[93] In doing so, policymakers would ensure that health care providers are required to clarify the types of services they do and do not provide and would allow for patients to enter these hospitals better informed. In addition, local policymakers should clarify and explicitly state that it is against federal law to deny emergency reproductive health care.[94] States should also require that hospital mergers and acquisitions retain vital health services, including reproductive health care.[95]

Prohibit For-Profit Business Corporations from Claiming Exemptions from Anti-Discrimination Laws

The Massachusetts No Excuses for Corporate Discrimination Act—also known as H. 767—attempts to provide a solution to businesses claiming religious or secular moral exemptions from anti-discrimination laws.[96] The bill, which is currently under consideration in the Massachusetts Legislature, would close the loophole that allows for-profit business corporations to use claims of religious freedom to challenge anti-discrimination law, which have only recently started to be successful following the 2014 *Hobby Lobby* decision.[97] H. 767 specifically applies to business corporations and not to nonprofit organizations, which include religious organizations. State law grants business corporations their existence, powers, and conditions of operations.[98] As a result, states have an opportunity to implement legislation to ensure that for-profit corporations are not using claims of religious freedom to justify discrimination. H. 767 also would protect people from being discriminated against on the basis of religion since, under current law, for-profit business corporations can discriminate against an individual during the hiring process only to claim later that the laws against discrimination in hiring do not apply because of the owner or corporation's religious beliefs. Overall, this bill attempts to ensure that anti-discrimination laws are not subject to corporate claims for exemptions based on religious or moral beliefs.

Extend Nondiscrimination Laws at the Federal Level

The passing of the recently reintroduced Equality Act would extend nondiscrimination laws at the federal level to apply to everyone, including LGBTQ people.[99] Seventy percent of Americans already agree that a federal law is necessary to protect LGBTQ people from discrimination in areas such as public accommodations, employment, housing, and credit.[100] The LGBTQ population has long been subject to discrimination on the basis of certain religious-based claims, and as a result, they should be included in specific nondiscrimination protections.

Consult Faith Communities in Local Policymaking and Foster Interfaith Dialogue

Local faith communities should be consulted in local policymaking in order to respond to their concerns and establish a formalized path of communication. For example, Maryland's Montgomery County Office of Community Partnerships houses the Faith Community Advisory Council (FCAC), which "ensures that the county executive is well informed of and able to act effectively in responding to the needs and concerns of faith communities, and to work collaboratively with government, nonprofits, and community organizations."[101] Through working groups like the Religious Land Use Working Group, the Faith Community Working Group, and the Neighbors in Need Working Group, the FCAC advises the county executive on the needs and concerns of members of the faith community in Montgomery County.[102] The council represents a diverse range of faith traditions in order to ensure that the many voices of the faith community are considered in policymaking. Other counties and local governments should adopt a similar working group model while also ensuring that less-often heard voices are included in policymaking decisions—such as those of atheists, women, LGBTQ people, and people of color.

As the Christian-identifying population in the United States declines and populations of those who identify as other faiths or are religiously unaffiliated grow, interfaith education and understanding become even more important.[103] Local governments have the opportunity to implement paths for interfaith involvement and consultation on local religious liberty-related issues.

Several state and local governments are also engaging faith leaders on local issues through the creation of interfaith task forces. For example, New York Governor Andrew Cuomo (D) created an interfaith advisory council to receive input on achieving greater interreligious understanding and promoting inclusivity and open-mindedness.[104] Meanwhile, in Maryland, the Governor's Office of Community Initiatives builds interfaith partnerships with local faith leaders and organizations on issues such as homelessness, poverty, and domestic violence prevention.[105] Groups like these should be consulted on addressing local interfaith issues—similar to how Atlanta Mayor Maynard Jackson (D) implemented the groundwork for an interfaith chaplaincy with the support of local, diverse clergy.[106] A successful interfaith task force should promote opportunities for listening and gathering. For example, the Interfaith Council of Southern Nevada's Mayors Prayer Breakfast gathers more than 500 civic and religious leaders to celebrate the region's diversity and explore solutions to community problems.[107] Local interfaith task forces provide an opportunity for consultation and engagement from local faith leaders and organizations, thus promoting an inclusive vision of religious liberty.

Conclusion

Administrative and legislative options exist at the federal, state, and local levels to ensure that religious liberty is not used as a justification for discrimination. Policymakers should ensure that laws like the Religious Freedom Restoration Act uphold the right to religious liberty while also ensuring that populations particularly vulnerable to the abuse of religious liberty are legally protected from such discrimination. This menu of policy options serves as a model to create and maintain protections ensuring that the original intentions of religious liberty are upheld. These policy options would protect many people from the potential harm of a warped application of religious liberty—particularly populations that are most vulnerable, such as women, people of color, religious minorities, and LGBTQ individuals.

Religious liberty must extend to the growing and changing diversity of the American public. Its misuse, currently spearheaded by the Trump administration, has prioritized certain political goals and religious beliefs and will have lasting impacts on houses of worship, religious institutions, the courts, and laws at the federal, state, and local levels. If policymakers do not ensure that religious liberty protects the free exercise of religion for all Americans, it will continue to be weaponized as a tool for discrimination and political gain and weaken nondiscrimination protections. Religious liberty must include everyone; it should not be a tool to ensure that only a specific set of religious beliefs and communities are prioritized above others.

Endnotes

1. Religious Freedom Restoration Act, Public Law 141, 103rd Cong., 1st sess. (November 16, 1993), available at https://www.govinfo.gov/content/pkg/STATUTE-107/pdf/STATUTE-107-Pg1488.pdf.

2. Ibid.

3. Sharita Gruberg and others, "Religious Liberty for a Select Few" (Washington: Center for American Progress, 2018), available at https://cdn.americanprogress.org/content/uploads/2018/04/03074429/ReligiousExemptions-report-5.pdf.

4. Don Byrd, "State RFRA bill tracker," Baptist Joint Committee for Religious Liberty, available at https://bjconline.org/staterfratracker/ (last accessed March 2019).

5. Donna Barry and others, "A Blueprint for Reclaiming Religious Liberty Post-Hobby Lobby" (Washington: Center for American Progress, 2014), available at https://cdn.americanprogress.org/wp-content/uploads/2014/07/ReligiousLibertyReport.pdf.

6. Gruberg and others, "Religious Liberty for a Select Few."

7. Ibid.

8. Barry and others, "A Blueprint for Reclaiming Religious Liberty Post-Hobby Lobby."

9. Emily London and Maggie Siddiqi, "Reclaiming Religious Freedom," Center for American Progress, February 5, 2019, available at https://www.americanprogress.org/issues/religion/news/2019/02/05/465814/reclaiming-religious-freedom/.

10. Pew Research Center, "America's Changing Religious Landscape," available at http://www.pewforum.org/religious-landscape-study/ (last accessed March 2019).

11. Ibid.

12. Robert P. Jones and others, "What It Means to Be American: Attitudes in an Increasingly Diverse America Ten Years after 9/11" (Washington: Governance Studies at Brookings and Washington: Public Religion Research Institute, 2011),

available at https://www.prri.org/wp-content/uploads/2011/09/Pluralism-2011
-Brookings-Report.pdf.

81. Robert P. Jones, "Fortnight of Facts: Is Religious Liberty Being Threatened in the US
Today?", Public Religion Research Institute, June 22, 2012, available at https://
www.prri.org/spotlight/fortnight-of-facts-is-religious-liberty-being-threatened
-in-the-u-s-today/.

82. Philip Schwadel and Gregory A. Smith, "Evangelical approval of Trump remains high,
but other religious groups are less supportive," Pew Research Center, March 18,
2019, available at https://www.pewresearch.org/fact-tank/2019/03
/18/evangelical-approval-of-trump-remains-high-but-other-religious
-groups-are-less-supportive/?utm_source=Pew+Research+Center&utm_
campaign=1b81451b07-83. RELIGION_WEEKLY_
CAMPAIGN_2019_03_20_02_31&utm_medium=email&utm_
term=0_3e953b9b70-1b81451b07-400474129.

83. Daniel Cox and Robert P. Jones, "Majority of Americans Oppose Transgender
Bathroom Restrictions" (Washington: Public Religion Research Institute, 2017),
available at https://www.prri.org/research/lgbt-transgender-bathroom
-discrimination-religious-liberty/.

84. CAP analysis of FBI, "2017 FBI Hate Crime Statistics," available at https://ucr.fbi.gov
/hate-crime/2017/topic-pages/tables/table-1.xls (last accessed March 2019).

90. Do No Harm Act, S. 593, 116th Cong., 1st sess. (February 28, 2019), available at
https://www.congress.gov/bill/116th-congress/senate-bill/593
/text?q=%7B%22search%22%3A%5B%22markey%22%5D%7D.

91. Rewire.News, "Texas Religious Freedom Restoration Act," available at https://rewire
.news/legislative-tracker/law/texas-religious-freedom-restoration-act/ (last
accessed March 2019).

92. Rewire.News, "Religious Freedom Restoration Act (RFRA)," available at https://
rewire.news/legislative-tracker/law-topic/religious-freedom-restoration-act/ (last
accessed March 2019); Texas Statutes, "Civil Practice and Remedies Code: Title
5. Governmental Liability, Chapter 110. Religious Freedom," available at https://
statutes.capitol.texas.gov/Docs/CP/htm/CP.110.htm (last accessed March 2019).

93. Washington State Legislature, "WAC 246-320-141: Patient rights and organizational
ethics," available at http://apps.leg.wa.gov/wac/default.aspx?cite=246-320-141 (last
accessed March 2019).

94. Kaye and others, "Health Care Denied."

95. Shepherd and others, "Bearing Faith."

96. *An Act to Strengthen Civil Rights*, H. 767, 191st General Court of the Commonwealth
of Massachusetts (2019-2020), available at https://malegislature.gov/Bills/191
/H767.

97. Free Speech for People, "Massachusetts No Excuses for Corporate Discrimination Act,"
available at https://freespeechforpeople.org/mass-no-religious-excuses-corporate
-discrimination-act/ (last accessed March 2019).

98. Ibid.

99. Equality Act, H.R. 5, 116th Cong., 1st sess. (March 13, 2019), available at https://www
.congress.gov/116/bills/hr5/BILLS-116hr5ih.pdf.

100. Harris Insights & Analytics, "'Open to All' Movement in the Post-Masterpiece Era."

101. Montgomery County Faith Community Advisory Council, "About Us," available at
http://montgomerycountyinterfaithmd.org/about/ (last accessed March 2019).

102. Montgomery County Faith Community Advisory Council, "Religious Land Use
Working Group," available at http://montgomerycountyinterfaithmd.org/about/

religious-land-use-working-group/ (last accessed March 2019); Montgomery County Faith Community Advisory Council, "Faith Community Working Group," available at http://montgomerycountyinterfaithmd.org/about/faith-community-working-group/ (last accessed March 2019); Montgomery County Faith Community Advisory Council, "Neighbors in Need Working Group," available at http://montgomerycountyinterfaithmd.org/about/neighbors-in-need-working-group/ (last accessed March 2019).

103. Pew Research Center, "America's Changing Religious Landscape."

104. John Woods, "Cardinal to Head Governor's Interfaith Advisory Council," Catholic New York, January 19, 2017, available at http://www.cny.org/stories/cardinal-to-head-governors-interfaith-advisory-council,14987.

105. Maryland Governor's Office of Community Initiatives, "Faith-Based Outreach," available at http://goci.maryland.gov/interfaith/ (last accessed March 2019).

106. The Pluralism Project, "Interfaith Airport Chaplaincy, Inc.," available at http://pluralism.org/promising-practice/interfaith-airport-chaplaincy-inc/ (last accessed March 2019).

107. Interfaith Council of Southern Nevada, "Mayors Prayer Breakfast 2018," available at http://interfaithsn.org/mayors-prayer-breakfast-2015/ (last accessed March 2019).

| *"Causing harm to others is not what religious liberty is about."*

The Religious Freedom Restoration Act Is Discriminatory, but It Can Be Fixed

Louise Melling

In previous viewpoints, we've seen that the national Religious Freedom Restoration Act of 1993 was supported by people on both sides of the political divide. In the following viewpoint, Louise Melling explains why it has come to be far more controversial—and what can be done about that. Louise Melling is deputy legal director at the American Civil Liberties Union and the director of the ACLU's Ruth Bader Ginsburg Center for Liberty.

As you read, consider the following questions:

1. The RFRA was originally intended to protect the rights of people of minority faiths. How, according to the author, was the law misused?
2. What examples does the author give of harms caused by current readings of RFRA?
3. How would the Do No Harm Act protect religious freedom without discriminating, according to the viewpoint?

"The Religious Freedom Restoration Act Is Discriminatory: Let's Fix It," by Louise Melling, The National Catholic Reporter Publishing Company, May 18, 2016. Reprinted by permission.

W hen Congress passed the Religious Freedom Restoration Act in 1993, the American Civil Liberties Union supported it because we believed it would provide important protections for people to practice their faith.

Having fought for religious liberty for decades, we were troubled that the interpretation of the Constitution at the time did not sufficiently protect minority faiths. Over the years, we have used the Religious Freedom Restoration Act to fight for religious rights, most recently on behalf of a Sikh student, Iknoor Singh, who was barred from entering the Army Reserve Officers' Training Corps unless he cut his hair, shaved his beard and removed his turban.

But today the Religious Freedom Restoration Act is being used as a vehicle for institutions and individuals to argue that their faith justifies myriad harms—to equality, to dignity, to health and to core American values. For example:

In 2014, a federal magistrate judge cited the Religious Freedom Restoration Act in ruling that a member of the Fundamentalist Church of Jesus Christ of Latter-Day Saints could not be required to cooperate in an investigation of child labor law violations. (Church leaders were accused of removing children from school and forcing them to harvest pecans on a private ranch, without pay, for eight hours a day.)

The Catholic Medical Association in Michigan is using the Religious Freedom Restoration Act to argue that Catholic hospitals cannot be required to provide abortions in case of emergencies. (The US Conference of Catholic Bishops claims that even though it receives federal money to provide services to unaccompanied immigrant minors, RFRA justifies its refusal even to inform unaccompanied immigrant minors who are pregnant that abortion is an option.)

Religiously affiliated nonprofit organizations recently argued before the Supreme Court that the Religious Freedom Restoration Act is violated if they are required to take the simple step of notifying the government that they object to providing insurance coverage for contraception to their employees. (On Monday, the court sent the case back down to lower courts to reconsider.)

Many states are looking to the Religious Freedom Restoration Act as a model for similar legislation, with proponents often saying the measure is necessary so anyone, including businesses, may for reasons of faith refuse to provide services for same-sex couples.

In all these cases, people suffer harm. Yet causing harm to others is not what religious liberty is about.

On Wednesday, May 18, Congress introduced legislation to fix the Religious Freedom Restoration Act—to bring the law back into line with its original intent. The "Do No Harm Act," if passed, would amend the Religious Freedom Restoration Act to ensure that federal law protects religious liberty but does not let religion be used—or misused—to harm others.

It would ensure that the Religious Freedom Restoration Act cannot be used to defeat protections against discrimination, to skirt wage and labor protections, to avoid compliance with laws protecting against child abuse, or to thwart access to health care guaranteed by law.

We recognize some people's heartfelt beliefs may conflict with the law. Business owners who believe marriage is the union between a man and a woman may not want to serve same-sex couples, and company owners may object to their insurer providing employees insurance coverage for contraception.

But our path forward may be easier if we look backward for guidance. In decades past, businesses and schools went to court to resist racial integration. Religious schools argued for the right to pay women less than men because, consistent with their faith, men were the heads of households. As a nation, we said no. Religion couldn't be used to discriminate and to harm a person's dignity, equality or opportunity.

The bill introduced in Congress today asks us to do the same. As Georgia Gov. Nathan Deal said in vetoing a state RFRA bill earlier this year, "I do not think we have to discriminate against anyone to protect the faith-based community."

> *"The government should not be permitted to coerce religious ministries like the Little Sisters of the Poor under threat of devastating fines."*

Obamacare Violates Religious Liberty

Sarah Torre

"Obamacare" is the term often used for the Affordable Care Act, legislation that, among other things, ensured that the majority of the population had access to health insurance. In the following viewpoint, Sarah Torre argues the law's requirement that insurance companies provide contraception services to insured parties violates the religious rights of employers. Sarah Torre is a policy analyst at the Heritage Foundation.

As you read, consider the following questions:

1. Why, according to the viewpoint, does Little Sisters of the Poor have a special reason to be exempted from the Obamacare mandate?
2. What is Little Sisters' particular objection to the mandate?
3. What is the problem with simply opting out of the program, according to the author?

"Religious Liberty at the Supreme Court: Little Sisters of the Poor Take on Obamacare Mandate," by Sarah Torre, The Heritage Foundation, March 22, 2016. Reprinted by permission.

O n March 23, the US Supreme Court will hear oral arguments from the Little Sisters of the Poor in their challenge to the Obamacare "contraception mandate," which threatens the sisters with crushing government fines unless—in direct violation of their religious beliefs—they facilitate coverage of abortion-inducing drugs and devices, contraception, and sterilization in their employer-provided health plan.

Dozens of religious nonprofits are challenging the Obamacare mandate, including charities, colleges and universities, religious high schools, missionary groups, and religious orders such as the Little Sisters of the Poor—an organization run by Catholic religious sisters dedicated to caring for the elderly poor. If religious nonprofit organizations fail to comply with the mandate, they face fines of up to $100 per affected employee per day.[1] For the Little Sisters, that could mean up to $70 million a year in federal fines, a devastating burden for a religious order with a long tradition of begging for food and donations to offset the costs of caring for the elderly poor.[2]

The mandate makes a serious assault on the fundamental freedom of individuals and organizations who form the backbone of civil society: those who care for the sick, feed the hungry, educate the next generation, and provide shelter and counseling for the most vulnerable Americans. The government should not be permitted to coerce religious ministries like the Little Sisters of the Poor under threat of devastating fines. The Supreme Court should rule against the Obama Administration and protect the religious freedom of the Little Sisters and other challengers.

Mandated Coverage of Abortion-Inducing Drugs and Devices

The Department of Health and Human Services (HHS) has used the health care law to require employers to cover, among other things, "the full range of Food and Drug Administration-approved contraceptive methods, sterilization procedures, and patient education and counseling for women of reproductive age."[3]

That list includes not only hormonal birth control and sterilization, but also "emergency contraceptives" like Plan B and *ella*, as well as intrauterine devices, which can sometimes prevent implantation of a living human embryo—effectively causing a very early abortion.[4] The Little Sisters of the Poor, like many religious organizations that believe life begins at conception, do not wish to be involved in providing coverage that includes life-ending drugs and devices and contraceptive methods.

The Mandate's Complicated Enforcement Mechanism

Only houses of worship and their "integrated auxiliaries" (like a church-run soup kitchen) are formally exempt from the mandate. For other clearly religious entities, like the Little Sisters of the Poor, the Obama Administration offers an alternative enforcement mechanism, which it concocted after nearly a dozen regulatory updates and hundreds of lawsuits over the rule.

Under the new rule, a religious nonprofit must either submit a "self-certification" form directly to its health insurer or third-party administrator (in the case of a self-insured plan) or send a notice letter directly to HHS with details and contact information about the organization's insurer or administrator. The former situation obliges the insurer or third-party administrator to provide coverage for the objectionable drugs, devices, and services.[5] In the latter situation, the government directs the insurer or third-party administrator to provide such coverage. In either case, the result is the same: After the nonprofit submits the form or letter, the employees enrolled in the health plan receive coverage that includes abortion-inducing drugs and devices, contraception, and sterilization at no cost to the insured.

Religious nonprofits challenging the mandate say that their participation in this scheme "authorizes, obligates, and incentivizes" their insurers to provide objectionable coverage and that this participation violates their sincerely held religious beliefs.[6] Indeed, in the case of a self-insured plan, submitting the self-certification form to the plan administrator would be effectively consenting to changing the terms of the contract to provide coverage, which the plan administrator is required to follow. Legal scholars have equated the scheme to a "permission slip" signed by religious institutions for insurers or administrators to provide abortion-inducing drugs and contraception.[7]

Even the government admits in the last two pages of its brief that under the law it cannot take over the religious nonprofit's health plans in this way *unless* the government receives identifying information about the organization's insurer or administrator. This is not a matter of simply opting out of the mandate. The government is forcing the Little Sisters and others, under threat of heavy fines, to furnish information that will trigger the inclusion of objectionable drugs and devices in their health plan in violation of their deeply held beliefs.[8]

Religious Freedom Restoration Act

The Little Sisters of the Poor and others challenging the coercive mandate argue that it violates the federal Religious Freedom Restoration Act (RFRA), which protects Americans' fundamental freedom from unnecessary government coercion. RFRA prohibits the government from doing anything that substantially burdens an adherent's religious exercise unless the government can demonstrate that it has a compelling interest and that its proposed action is the least restrictive way possible of achieving that compelling interest.

That is a high legal standard, one the federal government failed to meet during a 2014 case over the same HHS mandate involving Hobby Lobby, a family-run business. In that case, the Court ruled against the coercive mandate, finding that it placed a substantial burden on individuals' fundamental right to run their businesses in accordance with their faith.

The Little Sisters' Fight for Religious Freedom

The complicated alternative enforcement scheme created by HHS bureaucrats amounts to nothing more than a smoke screen. The government is still forcing some religious organizations to be involved in providing abortion-inducing drugs and devices, contraception, and sterilization while completely exempting other religious organizations. This does not meet RFRA's high standard.

The Mandate Imposes a Substantial Burden

The federal government's lawyers argue that the opportunity to submit the self-certification form or notice letter to HHS offers the equivalent of an "opt out" from the contraceptive mandate, and that there is therefore no substantial burden.[9]

But the religious organizations rightly counter that the rules simply provide "a mechanism for [the Little Sisters of the Poor] to *comply with*, not avoid, the mandate to which they object."[10] As explained above, by signing the form or sending a letter to HHS, the Little Sisters set in motion a process by which the government takes over their health plan infrastructure to provide coverage that includes abortion-inducing drugs and devices, contraception, and sterilization. The Little Sisters believe this makes them morally complicit in the provision of such drugs and devices.

Again, if religious nonprofits do not comply, they face serious and devastating fines. Being forced to choose between violating one's faith or facing government penalties is, the Little Sisters argue, "a quintessential substantial burden on religious exercise."[11]

The Government Has Not Shown a Compelling Justification for Burdening These Organizations in This Way

The government claims it has a compelling interest in ensuring that all women enrolled in a health plan have cost-free access to contraceptive drugs and devices because doing so would ensure "full and equal health coverage" for women and reduce rates of unintended pregnancy—a claim that is itself disputed.[12]

But the government's interest cannot be so important. It has exempted the health plans of tens of millions of employees from the contraceptive and abortion-inducing drug mandate for reasons ranging from the political to those of logistical convenience. Many large corporations—such as Visa, Pepsi Bottling, and Exxon—are exempt from the contraceptive mandate under the ACA's grandfather provision and the US military health plan is not required to cover the mandated drugs and services. Moreover, employers with fewer than 50 employees are not required to provide employee health coverage at all. In total, the health plans of about one in three Americans are effectively exempt from this mandate.[13]

More important, HHS has formally exempted houses of worship from the mandate because the government recognized that the mandated coverage could create conflicts of conscience for many religious institutions. Instead of broadly exempting religious organizations with objections to the mandate, HHS looked to an arcane IRS reporting provision that applies only to formal houses of worship in order to exempt the narrowest segment of religious institutions. Houses of worship do not have to fill out forms or even notify the government of their objection to providing coverage that includes some of these drugs and devices; they are automatically excluded—even if they do not actually object to any of the mandated coverage.

Hijacking Nuns' Health Plans Is Not Least Restrictive Means

Even if the government could show a compelling interest in ensuring cost-free access to contraception and sterilization, forcing the Little Sisters of the Poor to facilitate coverage that includes potentially life-ending drugs and devices is not the least restrictive means of achieving that goal.

As the Supreme Court noted in *Hobby Lobby*, and as the Little Sisters argue, there are other ways for the government to provide abortion-inducing drugs and devices and contraception to those who want them without hijacking employers' health plans and curtailing religious freedom.[14]

Writing for the majority in *Hobby Lobby*, Justice Samuel Alito wrote that the government could find a way to provide these services directly to women without entangling religious objectors.

If, as HHS tells us, providing all women with cost-free access to all FDA-approved methods of contraception is a Government interest of the highest order, it is hard to understand HHS's argument that it cannot be required under RFRA to pay *anything* in order to achieve this important goal.[15]

HHS Mandate's Assault on Religious Freedom

The cases before the Supreme Court are not about whether the Little Sisters or other religious nonprofits are correct in their religious beliefs. The Supreme Court has long recognized that judges are not competent to determine which beliefs are "good enough" for protection. After all, the right to the free exercise of religion includes the right to disagree with prevailing opinions.[16]

One need not agree with the Little Sisters' expression of their faith or share their opposition to abortion and contraception to recognize that the government should not force any American to violate his or her conscience in order to serve others, educate students, care for the sick, or comfort the dying.

All women, including those working for religious nonprofits, remain free to make their own decisions about the drugs and devices at issue in this mandate and to purchase or find coverage for them. A small number of charities, schools, and others are simply asking for the freedom not to be coerced into actively participating in a government-imposed scheme that their consciences do not allow.

Religious liberty can only be meaningful if it applies to everyone—not just those the government deems worthy.

The Supreme Court should rule against the Obama Administration's narrow view of faith and provide relief to the Little Sisters and other religious organizations from this coercive and unnecessary mandate.

Religion in Contemporary Society

Endnotes

1. Sarah Torre, "Obamacare's Fine on Faith: Trampling on Religious Liberty," Heritage Foundation *Issue Brief* No. 3553, March 27, 2012, http://www.heritage.org /research/reports/2012/03/obamacares-preventive-services-mandate-and -religious-liberty.

2. "Tradition of Begging," The Little Sisters of the Poor, http://www.littlesistersofthepoor .org/ourmission/tradition-of-begging (accessed March 21, 2016).

3. For more on the development of the HHS mandate, see Elizabeth Slattery and Sarah Torre, "Obamacare Anti-Conscience Mandate at the Supreme Court," Heritage Foundation *Legal Memorandum* No. 115, February 13, 2014, http://www .heritage.org/research/reports/2014/02/obamacare-anti-conscience-mandate -at-the-supreme-court, and Sarah Torre, "Obama Administration's Eighth Try on HHS Mandate and Religious Liberty Still Fails," The Daily Signal, August 22, 2014, http://dailysignal.com//2014/08/22/obama-adminstrations-eighth-try-hhs -mandate-religious-liberty-still-fails/.

4. Amici Curiae Brief of Association of American Physicians & Surgeons, et al. in *Zubik v. Burwell* (Nos. 14-1418, 14-1453, 14-1505, 15-35, 15-105, 15-119, 15-191).

5. 45 CFR §147.131.

6. Brief for Petitioners, p. 1, *Zubik v. Burwell* (Nos. 14-1418, 14-1453, 14-1505).

7. Joel Gehrke, "DOJ Asks Supreme Court Not to Block HHS Mandate for Little Sisters of the Poor," *Washington Examiner*, January 3, 2014, http://www .washingtonexaminer.com/doj-asks-supreme-court-not-to-block-hhs-mandate -for-little-sisters-of-the-poor/article/2541541 (accessed March 21, 2016), and "New SCOTUS Term: Win for Nuns on HHS Mandate?" *CBN News*, October 5, 2015, http://www1.cbn.com/cbnnews/us/2015/October/New-SCOTUS-Term -Win-for-Nuns-on-HHS-Mandate (accessed March 21, 2016).

8. Brief for Respondents, pp. 87–88 in *Zubik v. Burwell.*

9. Ibid., p. 13.

10. Brief for Petitioners, p. 42 in *Zubik v. Burwell* (Nos. 15-35, 15-105, 15-119, 15-191).

11. Ibid.

12. Brief for Respondents at 54 in *Zubik v. Burwell*; Michael J. New details counter-evidence to the government's claim that contraceptive coverage mandates will reduce unintended pregnancy rates in an amicus brief in *Zubik*, Brief for Amicus Curiae Michael J. New, Association Scholar, Charlotte Lozier Institute, in Support of Petitioners, *Zubik v. Burwell* (Nos. 14-1418).

13. "Understanding Who Is Exempted from the HHS Mandate," Little Sisters of the Poor .com, http://www.scotusblog.com/wp-content/uploads/2016/01/Little-Sisters -Merits-Brief.pdf (accessed March 21, 2016).

14. The government even admits in its brief that women without compliant health plans "will ordinarily obtain coverage through a family member's employer, through an individual insurance policy purchased on an Exchange or directly from an insurer, or through Medicaid or another government program." Brief for Respondents at 65 in *Zubik v. Burwell.*

15. *Hobby Lobby v. Burwell*, 573 US 41 (2014).

16. Ryan T. Anderson, "The Right to Be Wrong," *The Public Discourse*, July 7, 2014, http://www.thepublicdiscourse.com/2014/07/13432/ (accessed March 21, 2016).

Periodical and Internet Sources Bibliography

The following articles have been selected to supplement the diverse views presented in this chapter.

Bobby Allyn, "New York Ends Religious Exemptions to Required Vaccines," NPR, June 13, 2019. https://www.npr .org/2019/06/13/732501865/new-york-advances-bill-ending -religious-exemptions-for-vaccines-amid-health-cris

Nate Anderson, "Pharmacists with No Plan B," CatholicsforChoice .org, August 18, 2006. https://www.catholicsforchoice.org /pharmacists-with-no-plan-b/

Frederick Mark Gedicks, "Is Religion an Excuse for Breaking the Law?" *Newsweek*, March 12, 2016. https://www.newsweek.com /are-religious-beliefs-excuse-breaking-law-435664

Howard Gillman and Erwin Chemerinsky, "The Weaponization of the Free Exercise Clause," *Atlantic*, September 18, 2020. https://www .theatlantic.com/ideas/archive/2020/09/weaponization-free -exercise-clause/616373/

Tucker Higgins, "Supreme Court Shields Religious Schools from Discrimination Suits Brought by Teachers," CNBC, July 8, 2020. https://www.cnbc.com/2020/07/08/supreme-court-shields -religious-schools-from-discrimination-suits-brought-by -teachers.html

Lawrence Hurley, "US Supreme Court Delivers for Christian Conservatives in Trio of Rulings," Reuters, July 8, 2020. https:// www.reuters.com/article/us-usa-court-religion-rulings-analysis /u-s-supreme-court-delivers-for-christian-conservatives-in-trio -of-rulings-idUSKBN24932L

Lawrence Hurley and Jan Wolfe, "Next LGBT Legal Battle for Supreme Court Will Be Religious Exemptions," *Insurance Journal,* June 16, 2020. https://www.insurancejournal.com/news /national/2020/06/16/572333.htm

Scott Neuman, "Indiana's 'Religious Freedom' Bill Sparks Firestorm of Controversy," NPR, March 28, 2015. https://www.npr.org /sections/thetwo-way/2015/03/28/395987537/indianas-religious -freedom-bill-sparks-firestorm-of-controversy

Adam Sonfield, "In Bad Faith: How Conservatives Are Weaponizing 'Religious Liberty' to Allow Institutions to Discriminate," Guttmacher Institute, May 16, 2018. https://www.guttmacher .org/gpr/2018/05/bad-faith-how-conservatives-are-weaponizing -religious-liberty-allow-institutions#

Virginia Villa, "Most States Have Religious Exemptions to COVID-19 Social Distancing Rules," Pew Research Center, April 27, 2020. https://www.pewresearch.org/fact-tank/2020/04/27/most-states -have-religious-exemptions-to-covid-19-social-distancing-rules/

OPPOSING
VIEWPOINTS®
SERIES

CHAPTER 4

How Do You Define Religion?

Chapter Preface

In the previous chapters, viewpoint authors have expressed a variety of opinions about different aspects of religion in the modern world: the separation of church and state and the relationship between law and religious practice. But so far we have not heard any perspectives that discuss what religion is, and whether or not religion even requires a belief in a god.

In short, we have, for the most part, neglected the topic of atheism. Not too long ago, such an omission would have gone largely unnoticed. However, the ranks of non-believers is growing, whether they call themselves atheists, freethinkers, humanists, agnostics, or something else. That means that any discussion of religion needs to take into account those who have none or, as you will see later in this chapter, those who do have a religion but do not believe in a god.

Teasing out the many distinctions among what may loosely be called "non-believers" is a tricky matter. The first two viewpoints here, reports and analyses of surveys on religious belief in America, attempt to do that. That sets the stage for the rest of the viewpoints that approach the topic in a variety of ways. One author explains why he thinks that, contrary to what atheists say and even contrary to the definition of the word, atheism is a belief system. Another viewpoint explains what atheists, or at least most of them, do not believe (spoiler: that there is a god). One author reaches back in history to show that there need not be conflict between believers and non-believers. Atheists may not believe in God but can still be in favor of religion. The last viewpoint brings the chapter to a close with an essay that, perhaps, reflects the nebulous nature of this entire conversation. It asks if mystics are atheists.

> *"One-third of respondents ultimately say that although they do not believe in the God of the Bible, they do believe in a higher power or spiritual force of some kind."*

Americans Mean Many Different Things by "God"

Pew Research Center

Pollsters have collected a great deal of data that attempts to discern how many people believe in God or don't believe in God. However, those polls may not have much meaning if it is not clear what people mean when they answer the question. In the following viewpoint, the Pew Research Center attempts to get a better take on that important question. What they find is complicated. The Pew Research Center is a nonpartisan fact tank that informs the public about the issues, attitudes, and trends shaping the world.

"When Americans Say They Believe in God, What Do They Mean?" Pew Research Center, April 25, 2018. Reprinted by permission.

As you read, consider the following questions:

1. According to the viewpoint, what characteristics are shared by people who said they did not believe in the God of the Bible but did believe in some kind of higher power?
2. How many self-described atheists actually do believe in some kind of higher power?
3. What demographic groups were the least likely to say that they believed in the Biblical God?

P revious Pew Research Center studies have shown that the share of Americans who believe in God with absolute certainty has declined in recent years, while the share saying they have doubts about God's existence—or that they do not believe in God at all—has grown.

These trends raise a series of questions: When respondents say they don't believe in God, what are they rejecting? Are they rejecting belief in any higher power or spiritual force in the universe? Or are they rejecting only a traditional Christian idea of God—perhaps recalling images of a bearded man in the sky? Conversely, when respondents say they *do* believe in God, what do they believe in—God as described in the Bible, or some other spiritual force or supreme being?

A new Pew Research Center survey of more than 4,700 US adults finds that one-third of Americans say they do *not* believe in the God of the Bible, but that they do believe there is some other higher power or spiritual force in the universe. A slim majority of Americans (56%) say they believe in God "as described in the Bible." And one-in-ten do not believe in any higher power or spiritual force.

In the US, belief in a deity is common even among the religiously unaffiliated—a group composed of those who identify themselves, religiously, as atheist, agnostic or "nothing in particular," and sometimes referred to, collectively, as religious "nones." Indeed, nearly three-quarters of religious "nones" (72%) believe in a higher power of some kind, even if not in God as described in the Bible.

The survey questions that mention the Bible do not specify any particular verses or translations, leaving that up to each respondent's understanding. But it is clear from questions elsewhere in the survey that Americans who say they believe in God "as described in the Bible" generally envision an all-powerful, all-knowing, loving deity who determines most or all of what happens in their lives. By contrast, people who say they believe in a "higher power or spiritual force"—but *not* in God as described in the Bible—are much less likely to believe in a deity who is omnipotent, omniscient, benevolent and active in human affairs.

Overall, about half of Americans (48%) say that God or another higher power directly determines what happens in their lives all or most of the time. An additional 18% say God or some other higher power determines what happens to them "just some of the time."

Nearly eight-in-ten US adults think God or a higher power has protected them, and two-thirds say they have been rewarded by the Almighty. By comparison, somewhat fewer see God as judgmental and punitive. Six-in-ten Americans say God or a higher power will judge all people on what they have done, and four-in-ten say they have been punished by God or the spiritual force they believe is at work in the universe.

In addition, the survey finds that three-quarters of American adults say they try to talk to God (or another higher power in the universe), and about three-in-ten US adults say God (or a higher power) talks back. The survey also asked, separately, about rates of prayer. People who pray on a regular basis are especially likely to say that they speak to God and that God speaks to them. But the survey shows that praying and talking to God are not fully interchangeable. For example, four-in-ten people (39%) who say they seldom or never pray nonetheless report that they talk to God.

These are among the key findings of the new survey, conducted Dec. 4 to 18, 2017, among 4,729 participants in Pew Research Center's nationally representative American Trends Panel, with an overall margin of sampling error for the full survey of plus or minus 2.3 percentage points.

To explore the US public's beliefs about God, the survey first asked, simply: "Do you believe in God, or not?"

Those who said "yes"—80% of all respondents—received a follow-up question asking them to clarify whether they believe in "God as described in the Bible" or they "do not believe in God as described in the Bible, but do believe there is some other higher power or spiritual force in the universe." Most people in this group—indeed, a slim majority of all Americans (56%)—say they believe in God as described in the Bible.

Those who answered the first question by saying that they do *not* believe in God (19% of all respondents) also received a follow-up question. They were asked to clarify whether they "do not believe in God as described in the Bible, but do believe there is some other higher power or spiritual force in the universe" or, on the contrary, they "do not believe there is ANY higher power or spiritual force in the universe." Of this group, about half (10% of US adults) say they do not believe in a higher power or spiritual force of any kind.

All told, one-third of respondents ultimately say that although they do not believe in the God of the Bible, they do believe in a higher power or spiritual force of some kind—including 23% who initially said they believe in God and 9% who initially said they do not believe in God.

When asked additional questions about what they believe God or another higher power in the universe is like, those who believe in God as described in the Bible and those who believe in another kind of higher power or spiritual force express substantially different views. Simply put, those who believe in the God of the Bible tend to perceive a more powerful, knowing, benevolent and active deity.

For instance, nearly all adults who say they believe in the God of the Bible say they think God loves all people regardless of their faults, and that God has protected them. More than nine-in-ten people who believe in the biblical God envisage a deity who knows everything that goes on in the world, and nearly nine-in-ten say God has rewarded them, and has the power to direct or change everything that happens in the world.

Far fewer people who believe in some other higher power or spiritual force (but not the God of the Bible) ascribe these attributes and actions to that higher power. Still, even among this group, half or more say they believe another higher power in the universe loves all people (69%), is omniscient (53%), has protected them (68%) and rewarded them (53%).

Belief in God as described in the Bible is most pronounced among US Christians. Overall, eight-in-ten self-identified Christians say they believe in the God of the Bible, while one-in-five do not believe in the biblical description of God but do believe in a higher power of some kind. Very few self-identified Christians (just 1%) say they do not believe in any higher power at all.

Compared with Christians, Jews and people with no religious affiliation are much more likely to say they do not believe in God or a higher power of any kind. Still, big majorities in both groups do believe in a deity (89% among Jews, 72% among religious "nones"), including 56% of Jews and 53% of the religiously unaffiliated who say they do not believe in the God of the Bible but do believe in some other higher power of spiritual force in the universe. (The survey did not include enough interviews with Muslims, Buddhists, Hindus or respondents from other minority religious groups in the United States to permit separate analysis of their beliefs.)

When asked about a variety of possible attributes or characteristics of God, US Christians by and large paint a portrait that reflects common Christian teachings about God. For instance, 93% of Christians believe God (or another higher power in the universe) loves all people, regardless of their faults. Nearly nine-in-ten (87%) say that God knows everything that happens in the world. And about eight-in-ten (78%) believe God has the power to direct or change everything that goes on in the world. In total, three-quarters of US Christians believe that God possesses all three of these attributes—that the deity is loving, omniscient and omnipotent.

However, the survey finds sizable differences in the way various Christian subgroups perceive God. For example, while nine-in-ten of those in the historically black Protestant (92%) and evangelical (91%) traditions say they believe in God as described in the Bible, smaller majorities of mainline Protestants and Catholics say they have faith in the biblical God.[1] Sizable minorities of Catholics (28%) and mainline Protestants (26%) say they believe in a higher power or spiritual force, but not in God as described in the Bible.

Similarly, while about nine-in-ten adherents in the historically black Protestant tradition (91%) and evangelicals (87%) believe that God is all-loving, all-knowing and all-powerful, just six-in-ten Catholics and mainline Protestants say God possesses all three attributes.

Evangelicals and those in the historically black Protestant tradition are also more likely than members of other major US Christian traditions to say that God has personally protected, rewarded and punished them. But across all subgroups, Christians are far more likely to say God has protected and rewarded them than to say God has punished them.

Religious "Nones" Are Divided in Their Views About God

Seven-in-ten religiously unaffiliated adults believe in a higher power of some kind, including 17% who say they believe in God as described in the Bible and 53% who believe in some other form of higher power or spiritual force in the universe. Roughly one-quarter of religious "nones" (27%) say they do not believe in a higher power of any kind. But there are stark differences based on how, exactly, members of this group describe their religious identity.

None of the survey respondents who describe themselves as atheists believe in God as described in the Bible. About one-in-five, however, do believe in some other kind of higher power or spiritual force in the universe (18%). Roughly eight-in-ten self-described atheists (81%) say they do not believe in a higher power of any kind.

Self-described agnostics look very different from atheists on this question. While very few agnostics (3%) say they believe in God as described in the Bible, a clear majority (62%) say they believe in some other kind of spiritual force. Just three-in-ten say there is no higher power in the universe.

Respondents who describe their religion as "nothing in particular" are even more likely to express belief in a deity; nine-in-ten take this position, mirroring the US public overall in this regard. While most people in this "nothing in particular" group believe in a spiritual force other than the biblical God (60%), a sizable minority (28%) say they do believe in God as described in the Bible.

Young People Less Inclined to Claim Belief in Biblical God

Majorities in all adult age groups say they believe in God or some other higher power, ranging from 83% of those ages 18 to 29 to 96% of those ages 50 to 64. But young adults are far less likely than their older counterparts to say they believe in God as described in the Bible. Whereas roughly two-thirds of adults ages 50 and older say they believe in the biblical God, just 49% of those in their 30s and 40s and just 43% of adults under 30 say the same. A similar share of adults ages 18 to 29 say they believe in another higher power (39%).

The survey also shows that, compared with older adults, those under age 50 generally view God as less powerful and less involved in earthly affairs than do older Americans. At the same time, however, young adults are somewhat more likely than their elders to say they believe that they personally have been punished by God or a higher power in the universe.

Highly Educated Americans Less Likely to Believe in God of the Bible

Among US adults with a high school education or less, fully two-thirds say they believe in God as described in the Bible. Far fewer adults who have obtained some college education say they believe in God as described in the Bible (53%). And among college graduates, fewer than half (45%) say they believe in the biblical God.

The data also show that, compared with those with lower levels of educational attainment, college graduates are less likely to believe that God (or another higher power in the universe) is active and involved in the world and in their personal lives. For instance, while roughly half of college graduates (54%) say they have been rewarded by God, two-thirds of those with some college education (68%) and three-quarters of those with a high school education or less (75%) say this. And just one-third of college graduates say God determines all or most of what happens in their lives, far below the share who say this among those with less education.

Republicans and Democrats Have Very Different Beliefs About the Divine

Republicans and Democrats have very different notions about God. Among Republicans and those who lean toward the GOP, seven-in-ten say they believe in God as described in the Bible. Democrats and those who lean Democratic, by contrast, are far less likely to believe in God as described in the Bible (45%), and are more likely than Republicans to believe in another kind of higher power (39% vs. 23%). Democrats also are more likely than Republicans to say they do not believe in any higher power or spiritual force in the universe (14% vs. 5%).

Additionally, while 85% of Republicans believe God loves all people, eight-in-ten believe God is all-knowing, and seven-in-ten believe God is all-powerful; Democrats are less likely to express each of these views. Two-thirds of Republicans say they believe God possesses all three of these attributes, compared with roughly half of Democrats (49%). Republicans also are more likely than Democrats to say God has protected, rewarded or punished them.

Among Democrats, the survey finds big differences between whites and nonwhites in views about God. Most nonwhite Democrats, who are predominantly black or Hispanic, say they believe in God as described in the Bible, and seven-in-ten or more say they believe God is all-loving, all-knowing or all-powerful, with two-thirds ascribing all of these attributes to God. In these ways, nonwhite Democrats have more in common with Republicans than they do with white Democrats.

In stark contrast with non-white Democrats, just one-third of white Democrats say they believe in God as described in the Bible, while 21% do not believe in a higher power of any kind. And just one-in-three white Democrats say they believe God (or another higher power in the universe) is all-knowing, all-powerful and all-loving.

Endnotes

1. In this report, Protestants are categorized into one of three traditions (the evangelical Protestant tradition, the mainline Protestant tradition or the historically black Protestant tradition) based, as much as possible, on their denominational affiliation. For details on how denominations were categorized into traditions, see "Appendix B: Classification of Protestant Denominations" in Pew Research Center's 2015 report "America's Changing Religious Landscape."

> "Some people who describe themselves
> as atheists also say they believe
> in some kind of higher power or
> spiritual force. At the same time,
> some of those who identify with a
> religion ... say they do not believe
> in God."

Atheists Are a Complex Group

Michael Lipka

In the following viewpoint, Michael Lipka zeroes in on Americans who identify as atheists. The author uses polling data to argue that atheists are not nearly so monolithic a group as some may expect. In fact, as we saw in the previous viewpoint, some people who call themselves atheists actually do believe in some kind of higher power, just not a traditional God figure. And some are members of traditionally theistic religions. Michael Lipka is editoral manager of religion research at the Pew Research Center.

"10 Facts About Atheists," by Michael Lipka, Pew Research Center, November 5, 2015. Reprinted by permission.

As you read, consider the following questions:

1. What European country has the highest share of people who identify as atheists?

2. According to the viewpoint, some Catholics and Jews say they do not believe in God. What do you make of that finding?

3. The information reported on in this viewpoint was gathered by a telephone survey. Do you think that might have influenced people's answers to the questions? If so, in what way?

M easuring atheism is complicated. Some people who describe themselves as atheists also say they believe in some kind of higher power or spiritual force. At the same time, some of those who identify with a religion (for example, say they are Catholic or Jewish) say they do not believe in God.

One thing is for sure: Along with the rise of religiously unaffiliated Americans—many of whom believe in God—there has been a corresponding increase in the number of atheists. Here are some key facts about atheists in the United States and around the world:

1. The share of Americans who identify as atheists has increased modestly but significantly in the past decade.

Pew Research Center telephone surveys conducted in 2018 and 2019 show that 4% of American adults say they are atheists when asked about their religious identity, up from 2% in 2009. An additional 5% of Americans call themselves agnostics, up from 3% a decade ago.

2. The literal definition of "atheist" is "a person who does not believe in the existence of a god or any gods," according to Merriam-Webster.

And the vast majority of US atheists fit this description: 81% say they do not believe in God or a higher power or in a spiritual force of any kind. (Overall, 10% of American adults share this view.) At the same time, roughly one-in-five self-described atheists (18%) say they do believe in some kind of higher power. None of the atheists we surveyed, however, say they believe in "God as described in the Bible."

3. Atheists make up a larger share of the population in many European countries than they do in the US.

In Western Europe, where Pew Research Center surveyed 15 countries in 2017, nearly one-in-five Belgians (19%) identify as atheists, as do 16% in Denmark, 15% in France and 14% in the Netherlands and Sweden. But the European country with perhaps the biggest share of atheists is the Czech Republic, where a quarter of adults identify that way. In neighboring Slovakia, 15% identify as atheists, although in the rest of Central and Eastern Europe, atheists have a smaller presence, despite the historical influence of the officially atheist Soviet Union. Like Americans, Europeans in many countries are more likely to say they do not believe in God than they are to identify as atheists, including two-thirds of Czechs and at least half of Swedish (60%), Belgian (54%) and Dutch adults (53%) who say they do not believe in God. In other regions surveyed by the Center, including Latin America and sub-Saharan Africa, atheists generally are much rarer.

4. In the US, atheists are mostly men and are relatively young, according to the 2014 Religious Landscape Study.

About seven-in-ten US atheists are men (68%). The median age for atheists is 34, compared with 46 for all US adults. Atheists also are more likely to be white (78% vs. 66% of the general public) and highly educated: About four-in-ten atheists (43%) have a college degree, compared with 27% of the general public. Self-identified atheists also tend to be aligned with the Democratic Party and with political liberalism.

5. The vast majority of US atheists say religion is not too or not at all important in their lives (93%) and that they seldom or never pray (97%).

At the same time, many do not see a contradiction between atheism and pondering their place in the world. About a third of American atheists say they think about the meaning and purpose of life at least weekly (35%), and that they often feel a deep sense of spiritual peace and well-being (31%). In fact, the Religious Landscape Study shows that atheists are more likely than US Christians to say they often feel a sense of wonder about the universe (54% vs. 45%).

6. Where do atheists find meaning in life?

Like a majority of Americans, most atheists mentioned "family" as a source of meaning when Pew Research Center asked an open-ended question about this in a 2017 survey. But atheists were far more likely than Christians to describe hobbies as meaningful or satisfying (26% vs. 10%). Atheists also were more likely than Americans overall to describe finances and money, creative pursuits, travel, and leisure activities as meaningful. Not surprisingly, very few US atheists (4%) said they found life's meaning in spirituality.

7. In many cases, being an atheist isn't just about personally rejecting religious labels and beliefs.

Most atheists also express negative views when asked about the role of religion in society. For example, seven-in-ten US atheists say religion's influence is declining in American public life, and that this is a good thing (71%), according to a 2019 survey. Fewer than one-in-five US adults overall (17%) share this view. A majority of atheists (70%) also say churches and other religious organizations do more harm than good in society, and an even larger share (93%) say religious institutions have too much influence in US politics.

8. Atheists may not believe religious teachings, but they are quite informed about religion.

In Pew Research Center's 2019 religious knowledge survey, atheists were among the best-performing groups, answering an average of about 18 out of 32 fact-based questions correctly, while US adults overall got an average of roughly 14 questions right. Atheists were at least as knowledgeable as Christians on Christianity-related questions—roughly eight-in-ten in both groups, for example, know that Easter commemorates the resurrection of Jesus—and they were also twice as likely as Americans overall to know that the US Constitution says "no religious test" shall be necessary to hold public office.

9. Most Americans (56%) say it is not necessary to believe in God to be moral, while 42% say belief in God is necessary to have good values, according to a 2017 survey.

In other wealthy countries, smaller shares tend to say that belief in God is essential for good morals, including just 15% in France. But in many other parts of the world, nearly everyone says that a person must believe in God to be moral, including 99% in Indonesia and Ghana and 98% in Pakistan, according to a 2013 Pew Research Center international survey.

10. Americans feel less warmly toward atheists than they do toward members of most major religious groups.

A 2019 Pew Research Center survey asked Americans to rate groups on a "feeling thermometer" from 0 (as cold and negative as possible) to 100 (the warmest, most positive possible rating). US adults gave atheists an average rating of 49, identical to the rating they gave Muslims (49) and colder than the average given to Jews (63), Catholics (60) and evangelical Christians (56).

> *"Atheists themselves have a worldview based upon certain beliefs, such as the belief that the universe, including life, came about by natural processes."*

Atheism Is a Religion

Simon Turpin

Now that we've taken a look at who atheists are and the variable ways they define themselves, we turn to a perspective that states atheism should be regarded as a religion. In the following viewpoint, Simon Turpin lists seven reasons he believes atheists are more religious than they admit. Simon Turpin is the UK executive director of Answers in Genesis, a ministry helping Christians defend their faith.

As you read, consider the following questions:

1. How does the author define religion?
2. If the author is correct and atheism is a belief system (a belief that there is not a God as opposed to a belief in a particular God), then how do you think he would characterize agnostics?
3. Does using the Bible as support undermine the author's argument? Why or why not?

"Seven Ways Atheists Are Religious," by Simon Turpin, used by permission from Answers in Genesis, www.AnswersinGenesis.org.

Because of the secularization of the Western World, many people today now identify as not religious ("the nones"). In 2016 and 2017, according to some national surveys, 48.5% of people in England and Wales[1] and 72% of people in Scotland[2] say they have no religion! Many of these people identified as atheists. But are atheists not religious? Atheists will tell you they are not religious, but several characteristics identify atheists as religious. In this article, I deal with seven of those characteristics.

What Is Religion?

Before we look at seven of the characteristics that identify atheism as a religion, we need to ask the question: "What is religion?" It should be noted that it is particularly difficult to define religion as there is not a universally accepted definition. The Oxford English Dictionary defines religion as "the belief in and worship of a superhuman controlling power, especially a personal God or gods." Under this definition, atheism would not be viewed as religious since the dictionary definition of atheism is "disbelief or lack of belief in the existence of God or gods."

Yet, atheism isn't just a lack of belief in God (or gods). It was not a lack of belief in God that caused atheists to write books such as *The God Delusion* (Richard Dawkins), or *God Is Not Great* (Christopher Hitchens). Those books are designed to convince people that theism is false and that atheism is true. The Oxford English Dictionary also defines religion as "a particular system of faith and worship" and "a pursuit or interest followed with great devotion." Under that second definition of religion, atheism is religious. Many atheists (e.g., Richard Dawkins) spend much of their time railing against the Creator they believe doesn't exist, and they hold their cause with great devotion and faith.

I think that a better way to understand religion is as a system of belief: a person's ultimate standard for reality—their worldview. Atheists themselves have a worldview based upon certain beliefs, such as the belief that the universe, including life, came about by natural processes. This is a belief based upon faith: blind faith! It is nothing more than self-imposed worship—a secular religion (cf. Colossians 2:23).[3]

Seven Dimensions of Religion

A helpful way to know if a system of thought or worldview is religious is to look at the characteristics that most religions share. In his book *Dimensions of the Sacred*, the renowned anthropologist Ninian Smart set forth seven of these dimensions to detect whether something is religious:[4]

1. Narrative
2. Experiential
3. Social
4. Doctrinal
5. Ethical
6. Ritual
7. Material[5]

Let's just briefly consider each of these dimensions in light of the system of thought that is naturalistic atheism.

Narrative

Just about every religion has a narrative that explains the world around them. Briefly, the Christian narrative is creation, fall, redemption, and consummation, for example. In the Western World, the narrative of atheism used to explain the existence of life and the world around them is Darwinian evolution, and the philosophy that it entails. Richard Dawkins has famously said, "Darwin made it possible to be an intellectually fulfilled atheist."[6] The whole point of Darwinian evolution is to show that there is no need for a supernatural Creator.

The narrative of evolution and millions of years is not only an account of the origin of the universe but also about the end of it. Evolutionists, thus, have an eschatology (a belief about how the universe will end). In the narrative of evolution, the universe will finally come to an end in what naturalistic scientists call a "heat death."[7] Basically, the atheistic narrative begins with nothing, then something inexplicably appears, then life accidentally starts and evolves over billions of years, and ultimately everything will die, and there will be no more heat, energy, or motion left in the universe.

Experiential, Social, and Ritual

The experiential, social, and ritual aspects of atheism can be seen in the recent establishing of atheist churches. In an interview in the UK newspaper the *Telegraph* (October 2014), a leader of one of the first atheist churches said,

> The first event took place in the deconsecrated Union Chapel in London in July last year [2013]. Some 300 people attended the launch. A typical Sunday Assembly consists of a sing-along (pop songs rather than hymns), a secular reading, a talk that helps the congregation "live better, help often or wonder more"—the company's mantra—followed by a moment of reflection, then tea and cake.[8]

The atheist church "now exists in 55 outposts, across Britain, continental Europe, North America, and Australia, with a total of about 3,500 regular attendees … ."[9] It is interesting that the atheists chose to meet on a Sunday. But notice the leader of the atheist church said that their service includes a talk that helps people "live better, help often or wonder more."

One question that must be asked is, "live better than what?" This assumes an objective standard of morality, but atheism does not have an objective standard of morality (see below). One of the reasons atheists can talk about "living better" is, as recognised by historian Tom Holland (atheist/agnostic), that "modern atheism in the West is Christian atheism. And secularism and liberalism are shot through with Christian ethical and moral presumptions and understandings."[10] In other words, modern atheists borrow their moral standards from the Christian worldview. Nonetheless, what do atheists "wonder more" about? If life is meaningless and purposeless and if the history of the world is just "... full of sound and fury, but signifies nothing"[11] as some atheists claim, then what is there to wonder about in any objective sense? Atheism and the transcendent do not go together. The fact that atheists meet to do these things shows the reality of their religious behaviour.

Doctrine

Atheists even have doctrine and are evangelistic in their promotion of it. For example, a few years ago, the humanist society in the UK teamed up with atheist Richard Dawkins for a famous advertising campaign that they plastered on the side of buses that read, "There's Probably No God. Now Stop Worrying and Enjoy Your Life." The fact that atheists go out of their way to let other people know what they believe and even come up with principles to live life by (even called, for example, the "New Ten Commandments")[12] is evidence of their religion. Ultimately, if there is no God, why do the atheists spend so much of their time telling other people about it? Atheists don't spend the time and money to write books, have websites, and pay for advertising that argues against Santa Claus! From a Christian viewpoint, they are trying to supress the knowledge of God (Romans 1:18-20). But why the effort? This is surely a waste of the short time they have on this earth. If there is no life after death, then why not just ". . . eat and drink, for tomorrow we die." (1 Corinthians 15:32).

Ethical

Even though atheists are moral relativists, they make ethical claims. Many leading atheists have argued that Christian parents who raise their children according to their own faith are committing "child abuse." Atheist Daniel C. Dennett argues that many declare that "there is the sacred and inviolable right of life. … On the other hand, many of the same people declare that, once born, the child loses its right not to be indoctrinated or brainwashed or otherwise psychologically abused by those parents."[13]

But how can Dennett as an atheist even establish this ethical claim (of child abuse) when he has no foundation on which to make

More Than a Quarter of Americans Follow No Religion

The United States is becoming a less Christian country, and the decline in religious affiliation is particularly rapid among younger Americans, new figures show.

The proportion of US adults who describe themselves as Christian has fallen to two-thirds, a drop of 12 percentage points over the past decade, according to data from the Pew Research Center.

Over the same period, the proportion of those describing themselves as atheist, agnostic or "nothing in particular" has risen by 17 percentage points to more than a quarter of the adult population.

The proportion of US adults who are white born-again or evangelical Protestants—the religious group which strives hardest to see its political agenda adopted—is now 16%, down from 19% a decade ago.

The number going to church at least once or twice a month has fallen by seven percentage points over the past decade. More Americans now say they attend religious services a few times a year or less (54%) than say they attend at least monthly (45%).

The fall in religious identification and activity has affected both Protestant and Roman Catholic churches. According to Pew, 43% of adults identify with Protestantism, down from 51% in 2009. And 20% are Catholic, down from 23% in 2009.

absolute moral statements? Some leading atheist philosophers even admit that atheism implies amorality. Atheist Joel Marks, Professor Emeritus of Philosophy at the University of New Haven, states,

> The long and the short of it is that I became convinced that atheism implies amorality; and since I am an atheist, I must therefore embrace amorality. ... [T]he religious fundamentalists are correct: without God, there is no morality. But they are incorrect, I still believe, about there being a God. Hence, I believe, there is no morality.[14]

Atheists have no basis with which to question anybody's morality, given that they have no objective moral foundation on which to do so. Morality for an atheist is just a matter of opinion.

Fewer than half of millennials (49%) describe themselves as Christians; four in 10 are religious "nones," and 9% identify with non-Christian faiths.

Pew's report, released on Thursday, says the decline of Christian communities is continuing at a rapid pace.

"Religious 'nones' have grown across multiple demographic groups: white people, black people and Hispanics; men and women; all regions of the country; and among college graduates and those with lower levels of educational attainment.

"Religious 'nones' are growing faster among Democrats than Republicans, though their ranks are swelling in both partisan coalitions. And although the religiously unaffiliated are on the rise among younger people and most groups of older adults, their growth is most pronounced among young adults," the report said.

The share of US adults who identify with non-Christian faiths has increased from 5% in 2009 to 7% in 2019. Two percent of Americans are Jewish, 1% are Muslim, 1% are Buddhist, 1% are Hindu, and 3% who identify with other faiths, including people who say they abide by their own personal religious beliefs and people who describe themselves as "spiritual."

"Americans Becoming Less Christian as Over a Quarter Follow No Religion," by Harriet Sherwood, Guardian News & Media Limited, October 17, 2019.

From an evolutionary point of view, if humans are just evolved animals, then there is no such thing as absolute morality. Yet absolute morality is needed to make ethical judgements, such as child abuse, and the triune God of the Bible is needed to make absolute ethical judgements. Yet, many atheists are also more than happy to support abortion—the killing of a child in the womb—and argue that it is not child abuse.

This is not to say that you do not need to profess belief in God to argue morality, but you do need God to have absolute morality. In the Christian worldview, God is good and is the standard of goodness. So, apart from God any standard of our own making would be necessarily arbitrary, and ultimately self refuting.

Material

Finally, the material aspect of the religious nature of atheism can be seen in several ways, but specifically, it can be seen in the atheist's treatment of creation as sacred. In an interview in the UK newspaper *The Times* (April 2019), the founder of the global environmental movement "Extinction Rebellion" Gail Bradbrook, a molecular biophysicist, said,

> I don't believe in God, like there's some person there organising everything. I think there's something inherently beautiful and sacred about the universe and I think you can feel that just as well as an atheist. A bit of me thinks, "Is there a way to have some form of dialogue with the universe?"[15]

From an atheistic perspective, the universe does not care what you think, or how you feel. So, what would be the point of dialogue? In the US television program *Cosmos: A Space Time Odyssey*, astrophysicist Neil DeGrasse Tyson said of the stars,

> Our ancestors worshipped the sun. They were far from foolish. It makes good sense to revere the sun and stars because we are their children. The silicon in the rocks, the oxygen in the air, the carbon in our DNA, the iron in our skyscrapers, the silver in our jewellery—were all made in stars, billions of years ago. Our planet, our society, and we ourselves are stardust.[16]

According to Tyson, it was good, not foolish, that our ancestors worshipped the sun, even though God warns us not to worship creation and warns us of the folly of idolatry (Deuteronomy 4:19; Isaiah 44:9–20).[17] In this same episode Tyson also went onto say, "Accepting our kinship with all life on earth is not only solid science, in my view, it's also a soaring spiritual experience." As a naturalistic materialist, why is Tyson talking about a "spiritual experience"? Isn't it religious people who have "spiritual experiences"? Again, this is the inconsistency of the atheistic worldview, showing how religious the philosophy really is.

The Bible Identifies Atheists as Religious

Ultimately, it is the Bible that tells us atheists are religious. Whether it is through creation or conscience, the knowledge of God is revealed, and sinful men seek to suppress that which is revealed for their own purposes (Romans 1:18–20, 2:15). Atheists are not in a neutral position when it comes to the existence of God. God's creatures have no right in judging the existence of their Creator. The atheistic worldview ultimately ends up in irrationality because they have sinfully taken the truth about God's world and convinced themselves that it is not true.

Atheism is a false religion. It is the worship of self where they have ". . .exchanged the truth about God for a lie and worshiped and served the creature rather than the Creator" (Romans 1:25). The facts that (1) the leader of the atheist church wants to "live better, wonder more"; (2) Daniel Dennett believes child abuse is wrong; and (3) that Neil deGrasse Tyson can have a "spiritual experience" over creation all ultimately exemplify a recognition (whether they accept it or not) of what theologians call the sensus divinitatis (a true knowledge of God, i.e., Romans 1:18–23). It is to this sensus that Christians should appeal in order to show atheists the internal inconsistency of their own worldview. The reason that atheists can value and seek to preserve human life comes from the fact that knowledge of God comes to them not only through his creation but from the fact that they are made in his image (Genesis 1:27).

Atheism will be one of the many subjects that we will focus upon at our World Religions & Cults Conference in Oxford later this year. If you live in the UK or Europe, why not think about joining us and learn how to defend the Christian faith and share the gospel message effectively.

Endnotes

1. "People of no religion outnumber Christians in England and Wales—study," May 23, 2016, https://www.theguardian.com/world/2016/may/23/no-religion-outnumber -christians-england-wales-study.

2. "Majority of Scots say they are 'not religious,'" September 17, 2017, https://www.bbc .co.uk/news/uk-scotland-41294688.

3. In Colossians 2:23, the Greek word ethelothrēskia (self-made religion, ESV) is made up of two words: ethelo (will) thrēskia ("worship," "religion," "service"). It is probably best understood as worship freely chosen. See Douglas J. Moo, The Letters to the Colossians and to Philemon: Pillar New Testament Commentary (Grand Rapids, Michigan: Wm.B. Eerdmans Publishing, 2008), 240.

4. Not all of the seven dimensions are found in every religion.

5. For these criteria, see Ninian Smart, Dimensions of the Sacred: An Anatomy of the World's Beliefs (Harper Collins: London, 1996).

6. Richard Dawkins, The Blind Watchmaker (W. W. Norton, New York), 198.

7. See Andrei Linde, "Future of the Universe," in The Origin and Evolution of the Universe, eds. Ben Zuckerman and Matthew A. Malkin (Sudbury, Massachusetts: Jones and Bartlett, 1996), 128.

8. "Britain's 'atheist church' now pulls in crowds from Berlin to Ohio," 21st October 2014, http://www.telegraph.co.uk/finance/businessclub/11175092/Britains-atheist -church-now-pulls-in-crowds-from-Berlin-to-Ohio.html.

9. "What are atheist churches? Number of godless congregations growing across the Western world," May 21, 2018, https://www.theweek.co.uk/93733/what-are -atheist-churches.

10. Tom Holland said this at the "Hay Festival" in 2015 in the Q&A time after a lecture he gave entitled: "De-Radicalising Muhammad" (relevant section 49:27), https:// www.youtube.com/watch?v=I5slk97ss2Q.

11. See Atheist philosopher at Duke University Alex Rosenberg, The Atheists Guide to Reality: Enjoying Life Without Illusions (New York, New York: W. W. Norton & Company, 2011): 3.

12. In his book, The God Delusion, atheist Richard Dawkins cites the atheists "New Ten Commandments." 1. Do not do to others what you would not want them to do to you. 2. In all things, strive to cause no harm. 3. Treat your fellow human beings, your fellow living things, and the world in general with love, honesty, faithfulness, and respect. 4. Do not overlook evil or shrink from administering justice, but always be ready to forgive wrongdoing freely admitted and honestly regretted. 5. Live life with a sense of joy and wonder. 6. Always seek to be learning something new. 7. Test all things; always check your ideas against the facts and be ready to discard even a cherished belief if it does not conform to them. 8. Never seek to censor or cut yourself off from dissent; always respect the right of others to disagree with you. 9. Form independent opinions on the basis of your own reason and experience; do not allow yourself to be led blindly by others. 10. Question everything. See Richard Dawkins, The God Delusion (Great Britain: Bantam Press, 2006): 298–299.

13. Daniel C. Dennett, Breaking the Spell-Religion as a Natural Phenomenon (New York: Penguin Group, 2006): 326.

14. Joel Marks, "An Atheists Manifesto (Part 1)." Philosophy Now (August/September 2010). Marks does distinguish between hard atheists (himself) who believe in amorality and soft atheists (like Dawkins) who believe in morality.

15. "See Extinction Rebellion founder Gail Bradbrook: 'We're making people's lives miserable but they are talking about the issues,'" The Times, April 19, 2019, https://www.thetimes.co.uk/article/we-re-making-people-s-lives-miserable-but-they-are-talking-about-the-issues-d9hxcp53z.
16. See Ken Ham, "Students Told to Worship the Sun," January 27, 2015, https://answersingenesis.org/public-school/students-told-to-worship-sun/.
17. Idols were often representations of created things that were inaccessible to humans.

> *"To put it in a more humorous way:
> If atheism is a religion, then not
> collecting stamps is a hobby."*

Atheism Is Not a Religion

American Atheists

In the following viewpoint, American Atheists doesn't directly address the arguments made by Simon Turpin in the previous viewpoint, but it does explain what atheism is according to the organization. And by this definition, atheists cannot be said to have a belief system because atheism is defined not by a belief but by the lack of belief. American Atheists is an organization that supports religious equality for all Americans.

As you read, consider the following questions:

1. What, according to this viewpoint, is behind the common perception that atheism is a belief that there is not a God, rather than a lack of belief that there are gods?
2. Why does this viewpoint advocate using the word "atheist," rather than similar terms, such as "freethinker" or "humanist"?
3. How do the methods of the survey mentioned in this viewpoint differ from the ones used in the Pew studies discussed previously?

"What Is Atheism?" American Atheists, Inc. Reprinted by permission.

Atheism is one thing: A lack of belief in gods. Atheism is not an affirmative belief that there is no god nor does it answer any other question about what a person believes. It is simply a rejection of the assertion that there are gods. Atheism is too often defined incorrectly as a belief system. To be clear: Atheism is not a disbelief in gods or a denial of gods; it is a lack of belief in gods.

Older dictionaries define atheism as "a belief that there is no God." Clearly, theistic influence taints these definitions. The fact that dictionaries define Atheism as "there is no God" betrays the (mono)theistic influence. Without the (mono)theistic influence, the definition would at least read "there are no gods."

Atheism Is Not a Belief System Nor Is It a Religion.

While there are some religions that are atheistic (certain sects of Buddhism, for example), that does not mean that atheism is a religion. To put it in a more humorous way: If atheism is a religion, then not collecting stamps is a hobby.

Despite the fact that atheism is not a religion, atheism is protected by many of the same Constitutional rights that protect religion. That, however, does not mean that atheism is itself a religion, only that our sincerely held (lack of) beliefs are protected in the same way as the religious beliefs of others. Similarly, many "interfaith" groups will include atheists. This, again, does not mean that atheism is a religious belief.

Some groups will use words like Agnostic, Humanist, Secular, Bright, Freethinker, or any number of other terms to self identify. Those words are perfectly fine as a self-identifier, but we strongly advocate using the word that people understand: Atheist. Don't use those other terms to disguise your atheism or to shy away from a word that some think has a negative connotation. We should be using the terminology that is most accurate and that answers the question that is actually being asked. We should use the term that binds all of us together.

If you call yourself a humanist, a freethinker, a bright, or even a "cultural Catholic" and lack belief in a god, you are an atheist. Don't shy away from the term. Embrace it.

Agnostic isn't just a "weaker" version of being an atheist. It answers a different question. Atheism is about what you believe. Agnosticism is about what you know.

Not All Non-Religious People Are Atheists, But…

In recent surveys, the Pew Research Center has grouped atheists, agnostics, and the "unaffiliated" into one category. The so-called "Nones" are the fastest growing "religious" demographic in the United States. Pew separates out atheists from agnostics and the non-religious, but that is primarily a function of self-identification. Only about 5% of people call themselves atheists, but if you ask about belief in gods, 11% say they do not believe in gods. Those people are atheists, whether they choose to use the word or not.

A recent survey from University of Kentucky psychologists Will Gervais and Maxine Najle found that as many as 26% of Americans may be atheists. This study was designed to overcome the stigma associated with atheism and the potential for closeted atheists to abstain from "outing" themselves even when speaking anonymously to pollsters. The full study is awaiting publication in *Social Psychological and Personality Science* journal.

Even more people say that their definition of "god" is simply a unifying force between all people. Or that they aren't sure what they believe. If you lack an active belief in gods, you are an atheist.

Being an atheist doesn't mean you're sure about every theological question, have answers to the way the world was created, or how evolution works. It just means that the assertion that gods exist has left you unconvinced.

Wishing that there was an afterlife, or a creator god, or a specific god doesn't mean you're not an atheist. Being an atheist is about what you believe and don't believe, not about what you wish to be true or would find comforting.

All Atheists Are Different

The only common thread that ties all atheists together is a lack of belief in gods. Some of the best debates we have ever had have been with fellow atheists. This is because atheists do not have a common belief system, sacred scripture or atheist Pope. This means atheists often disagree on many issues and ideas. Atheists come in a variety of shapes, colors, beliefs, convictions, and backgrounds. We are as unique as our fingerprints.

Atheists exist across the political spectrum. We are members of every race. We are members of the LGBTQ* community. There are atheists in urban, suburban, and rural communities and in every state of the nation.

"*Though many today seem unaware of the fact, by no means all atheists have wanted to convert others to unbelief. Some have actually been friendly to religion.*"

Atheism Doesn't Have to Be Anti-Religious

John Gray

The previous viewpoint pointed out that atheism was lack of belief rather than a particular belief. In the following viewpoint, John Gray examines a question that often comes up when discussing atheism: Is atheism anti-religious? The author describes a type of atheism that is different from the sort made recently popular by atheists who spend a great deal of time criticizing Christian beliefs. Instead, he discusses two atheists from history who had very different approaches to their lack of belief. John Gray is an English political philosopher and regular contributor to the Guardian *and* New Statesman, *among other publications.*

"A Point of View: Does Atheism Have to Be Anti-Religious?" by John Gray, BBC News, August 30, 2015. Reprinted by permission.

As you read, consider the following questions:

1. How, according to the viewpoint, did Leopardi come by his views?
2. Why did Leopardi defend religion, even though he was a non-believer?
3. How were the views of the two men described in this viewpoint different from those of popular modern atheists, such as Richard Dawkins and Daniel Dennett?

In recent years we've come to think of atheism as an evangelical creed not unlike Christianity. An atheist, we tend to assume, is someone who thinks science should be the basis of our beliefs and tries to convert others to this view of things. In the type of atheism that's making the most noise today, religion is a primitive theory of how the world works—an intellectual error without human value, which we'd be better without.

But this isn't the only kind of atheism. History shows that atheism can have a complexity that reaches well beyond our currently dominant version. Though many today seem unaware of the fact, by no means all atheists have wanted to convert others to unbelief. Some have actually been friendly to religion. Nor have atheists in the past always turned to science for inspiration. There have been many varieties of atheism. That this has been so shouldn't be surprising. In itself, atheism is a purely negative position.

An atheist—and here I speak as one myself—is anybody who doesn't rely on an idea of God. Of course there are different ideas of God, but in western cultures the deity is understood as a divine mind that is all-knowing, all-powerful and all-loving. Atheists reject this idea, or simply don't need it. But that's all they have in common. Atheism has gone with a wide diversity of world-views and values. Among many atheists who differ from the present crop, let's look at two in particular.

Consider the early 19th Century Italian Giacomo Leopardi. Known chiefly for his exquisite verse, Leopardi was also a highly original thinker, who in his *Zibaldone*—a "hodge-podge of thoughts," some 4,500 handwritten pages long—produced a penetrating analysis of modern life. Brought up in a small hill-town to be a good Catholic by his father, an old-fashioned country nobleman who still wore a sword, Leopardi became an atheist in his teens.

For Leopardi, the universe was made of matter that obeyed physical laws. Humans were animals that had come into the world and acquired self-awareness by chance. Writing before Darwin, he didn't acquire this view of things from science, but from reading the classics and observing the life around him. Leopardi never renounced this uncompromising materialism. But at the same time he defended religion, which he regarded as an illusion that was necessary for human happiness.

If the modern world rejected traditional faiths, Leopardi believed, it would only be to take up others that were more harmful. He was not particularly fond of Christianity, whose claim to be a revelation for all of humankind he believed had led to intolerance. "Man was happier before Christianity," he wrote, "than after it." But the alternative to Christianity, in modern times, was what he called "the barbarism of reason"—secular creeds like Jacobinism in revolutionary France, which aimed to remake the world by force. These political religions would be even more intolerant than Christianity, Leopardi believed, and if you consider the history of the 20th Century, he was surely right.

Leopardi favoured the Catholicism in which he'd been brought up as the best available illusion. But he didn't return to religion himself. He spent his short life—born in 1798, he died in 1837—reading and writing, acquiring short-sightedness and a hunchback from spending so much time in his father's library. Sickly and poor most of the time, his principal human attachments were with a married woman and a male friend in whose house he died. He didn't share the illusions he believed were necessary to happiness, and much of his poetry has a melancholy tone. Yet he doesn't seem to have to been unhappy. His final hours were spent tranquilly dictating the closing lines of one of his most beautiful poems.

A quite different type of atheism was the driving force in the life of the essayist and novelist Llewelyn Powys. Born in 1884 as one of 11 children of a Somerset parson, two of whom—John Cowper Powys and Theodore Powys—also became well known writers, Llewelyn rejected the Christianity of his father with a fierce passion. Like Leopardi, he was a convinced materialist. Unlike Leopardi, he believed humankind would on the whole be better off if it renounced religion. But he didn't deny that religion contained something of value. "Sometimes, of an early Sunday morning," he wrote, "I would enter the old grey church to take the sacrament... And as I knelt with bowed head to partake of the beautiful, antique ritual I would try to conceive what inner secret the wild rumour held… I would feel half-inclined to believe also. Why not?"

As Powys saw it, the "wild rumour" of Christianity was like all religion—a response to the fact of mortality. For most of his adult life, he lived with death near at hand. In 1909, he learnt that he was suffering from tuberculosis. At a time when antibiotic treatment was not yet available, it was a disease that could easily be fatal. In fact Powys lived on another 30 years, never free of sickness, but determined to make the best of a life that would always be in danger.

Entering a Swiss sanatorium in 1910 for just over a year, he used his time there to throw off the timid morality in which he had been reared. Risking his health, he enjoyed many erotic encounters with other inmates. In a diary he kept, he recorded a haemorrhage that almost killed him, marking the episode in his own blood. As he wrote later in a memoir of his illness: "Presently, with the pretty egotism of youth, I dipped my fountain pen into the basin at my bedside and scratched a red cross on my diary, a cross such as a tramp might have made who could not sign his name, and yet who wanted to record some important event in his wayfaring." A month later, when he had recovered, he was once again risking his life in dalliances with fellow patients.

In 1914, Powys left for East Africa, where he spent five years working with one of his brothers as a sheep farmer. The harsh realities of life in the bush fortified his brand of atheism. Writing after his return, he declared that Africa "laps up the life-blood of all the delicate illusions that have for so long danced before the eyes of men and made them happy. Truth alone is left alive. What was suspected in Europe is made plain here… the surface is everything, underneath is nothing." He wasn't disconcerted at this discovery. He was clear that human life had no intrinsic meaning or purpose, but that only made him all the more determined to savour the sensation of being alive. As a freelance writer he was never financially secure and often hard-up. But accompanied in later years by his devoted partner, Alyse Gregory, he travelled widely, visiting the West Indies, Palestine, America and Capri, among other places.

Powys chose to live as a hedonist. Always close to death, he aimed to heighten the sensation of life. He attached as much importance to the contemplation of landscape and wild animals as he did to sexual pleasure. His essays are full of images of natural beauty—a hare drinking from a small pond, fox cubs playing at dawn on the Dorset cliffs. A week before he died of a perforated ulcer in Switzerland in December 1939, he wrote to a friend: "I have had a happy life for half a century in sunshine."

The two atheists I've discussed were very different from one another. Where Leopardi accepted a godless universe with tranquil resignation, Powys embraced it with exultant joy. But for both of them, religion was much more than an outdated theory. If Leopardi believed religion of one sort or another was beneficial for human happiness, Powys valued religion as a kind of poetry, which fortified the human spirit in the face of death.

But each of these atheists was also very different from most of the unbelievers of recent years. The predominant strand of contemporary unbelief, which aims to convert the world to a scientific view of things, is only one way of living without an idea of God. It's worth looking back to other kinds of atheism, far richer and subtler than the version we're familiar with, that aren't just evangelical religion turned upside down.

> "*The apophatic approaches would say that anything that one says about God is* not *God at all. That God doesn't exist, they say, and so they might be called 'atheistic.'*"

The God That You Can Name Does Not Exist

Bryce Haymond

In the following viewpoint, Bryce Haymond responds to a comment made by John Gray, the author of the previous viewpoint and Seven Types of Atheism. *Gray said mysticism was a type of atheism. The author of this viewpoint found that surprising and responded with this essay, in which in the final analysis says that God is ultimately unknowable by means of religion and can only be known by direct experience. Bryce Haymond is a writer, contemplative, and mystic.*

As you read, consider the following questions:

1. What does John Gray mean by "ineffable," and is that consistent or inconsistent with a belief in God?
2. How does the author describe God? Is that a typical view of God?
3. The viewpoint argues that religions tend to worship their images of God. What examples does the author give?

I n an interview with John Gray about his book *Seven Types of Atheism*, this exchange took place:

> *[Questioner:]* You finish with the mystical kind of atheism. It sounds almost like people who have a big drug experience and talk about the oneness of everything.
>
> *[Gray:]* Well, it's a radical kind of atheism that asserts that the nature of reality is ineffable—it can't be embodied in words. Schopenhauer thought the ultimate reality of things was spiritual, but we couldn't really grasp it with our reasoning. He didn't have any need for a creator God, but actually, he isn't so far from certain traditions in mysticism and different religions. Some types of mystical religion come close to atheism in their understanding of God as unimaginable.

What did he mean that some "mystical religion is close to atheism"? Aren't mystics supposed to be people who find union with God, who become one with God? How could that possibly be "atheistic"? Here is my interpretation.

God cannot be thought of in any absolute sense. Any words that we use to describe God can only point to God, but aren't God.

God is unimaginable because God must be experienced to be known. No amount of words will do it. Mystics and philosophers for centuries have tried to describe God, but all such descriptions fall short, and the wise know it. It is also the reason there are innumerable different descriptions of God. Each is trying to grasp that which is fundamentally beyond intellectual grasping, and they naturally use the symbols and knowledge from their own particular culture to grasp at it.

It is only through direct experience of God in one's own Being that we can come to "know" anything absolute about God, but that absoluteness cannot be communicated. It cannot even be known in the experiencer, in the traditional sense, in terms of thoughts. It is a direct, real-time, present, transcendent experience. As soon as the experiencer tries to put words or even thoughts to that experience, they are translating and interpreting it, and it becomes something *different* than what it was, which was pure experience.

God is not an idea, concept, thought, word, image, or symbol. God is relational, experiential, being, presence, awareness, love, reality, and truth. And yet even these words fall short, because they only provoke preconceived ideas in our minds, but not the direct experience of them.

The apophatic approaches would say that anything that one says about God is *not* God at all. *That* God doesn't exist, they say, and so they might be called "atheistic." Those words are only symbols *pointing* to the real God. But symbols are not God. Only *God* is God.

This led the Christian mystic Meister Eckhart, for example, to exclaim, "I pray God to rid me of God." All our preconceived ideas of God dissolve in the direct apprehension of that Ultimate Reality which we have given the linguistic label of "God." In a very real sense, we must give up or surrender all our ideas of God to know God, for God surpasses all our mere intellectual ideas.

And yet those ideas find new application in our experience, profound truth and meaning. It's not that those ideas are wrong so much as they are terribly incomplete and misleading without *experience*, often causing us to stop short and idolize the symbols of God rather than commune with God in reality.

Many mystics might be described as "atheists" of the Gods described by the religions, because they know God cannot be accurately described, *ever*, by anyone. They don't believe in *those* Gods. No descriptions of God suffice to define what God is so that we may truly know God. We must *experience* God to "know" God.

From my own Mormon background, in Joseph Smith's first ecstatic experience of God he recalled God saying:

> ...the world lieth in sin at this time and none doeth good no not one they have turned aside from the gospel and keep not <my> commandments they draw near to me with their lips while their hearts are far from me...

Smith realized that all religious doctrines that were being taught were wrong, they were incomplete, they were fallible, they were corrupt, they attempted to draw near to God with flowery and ornate words, but their hearts remained far from God. In that moment we could say that Smith became an "atheist" of all existent religious sects; he didn't believe in them, or the God they described. The God he had *experienced* was not there.

Another example comes from Yogananda's guru, Babaji, who had a vision of Jesus. It was a similar message:

> My followers have forgotten the art of divine inner communion. Outwardly they do good works, but they have lost sight of the most important of my teachings, to seek the Kingdom of God first.

Babaji discovered that the way the religions approached the Divine had been corrupted, they had lost the *experience* of communion with God. Babaji became a kind of "atheist" or unbeliever of their descriptions and teachings of God, having lost sight of the most important thing—*experience.*

Unfortunately, what often happens is that mystics who have such experiences of God then begin to interpret and translate their own experiences of God, whose words then eventually become the de facto way that God is, rather than the *experience*, and the process repeats itself. Thus we see religions that branch throughout history into new religions, each trying to better describe God, and each failing to do so.

The religions tend to worship their descriptions and images, like the Israelites worshiped the Golden Calf, while the mystics, sages, saints, and prophets commune with God directly. They know God far surpasses all such descriptions, and if one wants to know God, one must come into direct personal communion with God. All else is mythology, fallible, incomplete, symbolic, pointer, metaphor, etc. Those may be helpful guides, but they must be remembered that they are guides, and not the actual thing.

The wisest teachers help guide others to knowing God themselves through *direct experience*, because they know that nothing else can replace that direct personal first-hand knowing.

One of the greatest obstacles to knowing God is thinking one already knows God because of all of one's "book" knowledge about

God, all of the thoughts and ideas that fill one's mind about God, all the things that have been said about God that one has learned from others. But until one experiences God directly, one does not know God. One only knows the symbols that have been used to try to point towards God, but one does not know God as God is. Knowing God is different than knowing *about* God.

The God that one thinks one knows almost certainly *does not exist*. Direct experience abolishes all such thoughts, all such knowledge, all such images and symbols, in the direct perception of that Absolute Truth which is forever beyond our intellectual grasp.

Periodical and Internet Sources Bibliography

The following articles have been selected to supplement the diverse views presented in this chapter.

Sebastian Anthony, "Richard Dawkins Gives Science a Bad Name, Say Fellow UK Scientists," Ars Technica, November 1, 2016. https://arstechnica.com/science/2016/11/richard-dawkins-gives-science-a-bad-name-say-fellow-uk-scientists/

Lee Billings, "Atheism Is Inconsistent with the Scientific Method, Prizewinning Physicist Says," *Scientific American*, March 20, 2019. https://www.scientificamerican.com/article/atheism-is-inconsistent-with-the-scientific-method-prizewinning-physicist-says/

Nylah Burton, "How Some Black Americans Are Finding Solace in African Spirituality," Vox, July 31, 2020. https://www.vox.com/2020/7/31/21346686/orisha-yoruba-african-spirituality-covid

Tara Isabella Burton, "What Do Millennials Want from Religion: Three Shows Have the Answer," *The Jesuit Review*, July 25, 2019. https://www.americamagazine.org/arts-culture/2019/07/25/what-do-millennials-want-religion-three-shows-have-answer

Daniel Cox and Amelia Thomson-DeVeaux, "Millennials Are Leaving Religion and Not Coming Back," FiveThirtyEight, December 12, 2019. https://fivethirtyeight.com/features/millennials-are-leaving-religion-and-not-coming-back/

Mark Elliott, "What Place Is There for Religion in Modern Life?" The Conversation, May 26, 2016. https://theconversation.com/what-place-is-there-for-religion-in-modern-life-60026

Pavithra Mohan, "The US Is Less Religious Now: Are We Richer for It?" Fast Company, May 23, 2019. https://www.fastcompany.com/90350554/the-u-s-is-less-religious-now-are-we-richer-for-it

Rabbi Barry Silver, "A Rabbi Responds to the Four Horsemen of Atheism," *South Florida Sun Sentinel*, May 28, 2019. https://www.sun-sentinel.com/florida-jewish-journal/opinion/fl-jj-opinion-silver-rabbi-responds-four-horsemen-atheism-20190605-20190528-aq5om3yemrea3cm6zriykpkyve-story.html

David Smith, "'I Prefer 'Non-Religious': Why So Few US Politicians Come Out as Atheists," *Guardian*, August 3, 2019. https://www.theguardian.com/world/2019/aug/03/athiesm-us-politics-2020-election-religious-beliefs

Derek Thompson, "How America Lost Its Religion," *Atlantic*, September 26, 2019. https://www.theatlantic.com/ideas/archive/2019/09/atheism-fastest-growing-religion-us/598843/

For Further Discussion

Chapter 1

1. The author of viewpoint 2 argues that the founders of the nation took pains to make sure America had no official religion. Can you think of other nations that do have official religions? What are the consequences, both political and social, for these nations?
2. Thomas Jefferson and several other Founding Fathers were not Christians, but Deists. What is a Deist and how might their beliefs have influenced their thinking about the relationship between religion and government?
3. In viewpoint 3, the author says that the United States is not a Christian nation, but a free nation. What do you think he means by that? How might that statement be interpreted differently by a Christian living in the United States versus an American of a different, or no, religion?

Chapter 2

1. Should religious leaders avoid speaking out about politics? The US civil rights movement was largely spearheaded by churches and religious leaders. Does knowing this alter your opinion?
2. Health care providers are typically people of science, but they have religious views as well. In this chapter, we saw how those can sometimes come into conflict. Can you think of other examples? Draw on current events or your imagination.
3. Can you think of ways that a health care worker might approach a situation in which their obligation to give care conflicts with their religious beliefs? What might they do in such a situation to protect their own conscience while not harming someone who has different beliefs?

Chapter 3

1. The author of viewpoint 2 expresses concern that the *Hobby Lobby* case and RFRA laws are thinly disguised attempts to give corporations protections that are meant for individuals and thereby a license for them to use their power in a dangerous way. Do you think giving corporations legal status as personas is a potential problem? Why or why not?

2. When the federal RFRA law was first passed, it enjoyed bipartisan support across a wide spectrum of political and social communities. As you can see in this chapter, it soon lost much of that support. What happened?

3. Most of the viewpoints in this chapter found one or another reason to oppose, or at least tweak, RFRA laws, and most were concerned with the *Hobby Lobby* case. Can you think of a situation in which RFRA laws might be used fairly?

Chapter 4

1. The Pew survey in this chapter broke down belief in God or a higher power by demographic groups. Were you surprised by the results? Did you see any inconsistencies among the responses?

2. In this chapter, you saw the argument that belief in God or adherence to a particular religious belief system is not necessary for ethical behavior. Do you agree? What would you say *is* necessary for ethical behavior?

3. Considering the social and political climate of the United States, do you think the actual number of people who are atheists or agnostics might be larger than surveys show? Why or why not?

Organizations to Contact

The editors have compiled the following list of organizations concerned with the issues debated in this book. The descriptions are derived from materials provided by the organizations. All have publications or information available for interested readers. The list was compiled on the date of publication of the present volume; the information provided here may change. Be aware that many organizations take several weeks or longer to respond to inquiries, so allow as much time as possible.

Alliance Defending Freedom

15100 North 90th Street
Scottsdale, AZ 85260
(480) 444-0020
email: Contact via website form
website: www.Adflegal.org

The ADF is an organization of Christian leaders dedicated to defending the religious freedom of Christians in the United States. In addition to fighting in court, the organization attempts to change American culture in a way that supports Christian values.

American Atheists

225 Cristiani Street
Cranford, NJ 07016
(908) 276-7300
email: Contact via website form
website: www.atheists.org

This organization works to create a society in which casual bigotry against non-believers is unacceptable. It supports a world in which public policy is made using the best available evidence rather than religious dogma.

American Civil Liberties Union (ACLU)

125 Broad Street, 18th Floor
New York, NY 10001
(212) 549-2500
email: Contact via website form
website: www.aclu.org

The ACLU, founded in 1920, has spent almost a century defending and protecting the individual rights and liberties that are guaranteed by the Constitution of the United States, including the freedom of religion.

American Friends Service Committee

1501 Cherry Street
Philadelphia, PA 19102
(215) 241-7000
email: Contact via website form
website: www.afsc.org

Founded in 1917, the AFSC works with people from many religious and cultural backgrounds to promote lasting peace and justice. The organization supports respect for human life and the kind of change that transforms social relationships and social systems.

B'nai B'rith International

1120 20th Street NW, Suite 300N
Washington, DC 20036
(202) 857-6600
email: info@bnaibrith.org
website: www.bnaibrith.org

This international organization is the largest and oldest Jewish service organization in the world. It is dedicated to advancing human rights, advocating for Israel and global Jewry, and working to make the world a more humane and tolerant place.

Buddhist Peace Fellowship

PO Box 3470
Berkeley, CA 94703
(510) 239-3764
email: info@bpf.org
website: www.bpf.org
The Buddhist Peace Fellowship shares spiritual-political practices and resources to advance the cause of social justice. The BPF is made of people from multiple Buddhist lineages who seek to build a world where people take care of one another and use fierce compassion to heal systemic harm.

Catholic Extension

150 South Wacker Drive, Suite 2000
Chicago, IL 60606
(800) 842-7804
email: info@catholicextension.org
website: www.catholicextension.org

Catholic Extension works with America's poorest communities to transform lives and hearts. It provides funds and resources to invest in programs that support people, communities, and ministries.

Freedom from Religion Foundation

PO Box 750
Madison, WI 53701
(608) 256-8900
email: Contact via website form
website: www.ffrf.org

The Freedom from Religion Foundation is an organization dedicated to protecting the separation of church and state. It educates the public on matters relating to nontheism.

Southern Christian Leadership Conference

320 Auburn Avenue NE
Atlanta, GA 30303
(404) 522-1420
email: Contact@nationalsclc.org
website: www.nationalsclc.org

The SCLC is a civil rights organization born of the Montgomery Bus Boycott and still active today.

Teaching Tolerance

400 Washington Avenue
Montgomery, AL 36104
(888) 414-7752
website: www.tolerance.org

A project of the Southern Poverty Law Center, with an emphasis on social justice and inclusiveness, Teaching Tolerance provides teaching resources and information to help schools prepare students to be active and effective members of a diverse democracy.

Bibliography of Books

Christopher Cameron. *Black Freethinkers: A History of African American Secularism*. Chicago, IL: Northwestern University Press, 2019.

John Corrigan, et al. *Religion in America* (9th ed.). New York, NY: Routledge, 2018.

Caleb Iyer Elfenbein. *Fear in Our Hearts: What Islamophobia Tells Us About America*. New York, NY: NYU Press, 2021.

Gregg L. Frazer. *The Religious Beliefs of America's Founders: Reason, Revelation, and Revolution*. Lawrence, KS: University Press of Kansas, 2014.

Nile Green. *Global Islam: A Very Short Introduction*. Oxford, UK: Oxford University Press, 2020.

Mark David Hall. *Did America Have a Christian Founding? Separating Modern Myth from Historical Truth*. Nashville, TN: Thomas Nelson, 2019.

Sam Harris. *Waking Up: A Guide to Spirituality Without Religion*. New York, NY: Simon and Schuster, 2014.

Nazita Lajevardi. *Outsiders at Home: The Politics of American Islamaphobia*, Cambridge, UK: Cambridge University Press, 2020.

Esau McCaulley. *Reading While Black: African American Biblical Interpretation as an Exercise in Hope*. Downers Grove, IL: IVP Academic, 2020.

Roger L. Price. *When Judaism Meets Science*. Eugene, OR: Wipf and Stock, 2019.

Jonathan D. Sarna. *American Judaism: A History* (2nd ed.). New Haven, CT: Yale University Press, 2019.

Andrew L. Seidel. *The Founding Myth: Why Christian Nationalism Is Un-American*. New York, NY: Sterling, 2019.

Kenneth D. Wald and Allison Calhoun-Brown. *Religion and Politics in the United States* (8th ed.). Lanham, MD: Rowman and Littlefield, 2018.

Andrew L. Whitehead and Samuel L. Perry. *Taking America Back for God: Christian Nationalism in the United States.* Oxford, UK: Oxford University Press, 2020.

Pamela Ayo Yetunde and Cheryl A. Giles (eds.). *Black and Buddhist: What Buddhism Can Teach Us About Race, Resilience, Transformation, and Freedom.* Boulder, CO: Shambala, 2020.

Index